# Harvard
# Business
# Review

ON

ENTREPRENEURSHIP

# THE HARVARD BUSINESS REVIEW PAPERBACK SERIES

The series is designed to bring today's managers and professionals the fundamental information they need to stay competitive in a fast-moving world. From the preeminent thinkers whose work has defined an entire field to the rising stars who will redefine the way we think about business, here are the leading minds and landmark ideas that have established the *Harvard Business Review* as required reading for ambitious businesspeople in organizations around the globe.

Other books in the series:

*Harvard Business Review on the Business Value of IT*

*Harvard Business Review on Change*

*Harvard Business Review on Knowledge Management*

*Harvard Business Review on Leadership*

*Harvard Business Review on Managing People*

*Harvard Business Review on Managing Uncertainty*

*Harvard Business Review on Measuring Corporate Performance*

*Harvard Business Review on Nonprofits*

*Harvard Business Review on Strategies for Growth*

# Harvard Business Review

## ON

## ENTREPRENEURSHIP

A HARVARD BUSINESS REVIEW PAPERBACK

The *Harvard Business Review* articles in this collection are available as individual reprints. Discounts apply to quantity purchases. For information and ordering, please contact Customer Service, Harvard Business School Publishing, Boston, MA 02163. Telephone: (617) 783-7500 or (800) 988-0886, 8 A.M. to 6 P.M. Eastern Time, Monday through Friday. Fax: (617) 783-7555, 24 hours a day. E-mail: custserv@hbsp.harvard.edu

**Library of Congress Cataloging-in-Publication Data**
Harvard business review on entrepreneurship.
     p.   cm.—(A Harvard business review paperback)
    Includes index.
    ISBN 0-87584-910-5 (alk. paper)
    1. New business enterprises—Management.   2. Entrepreneurship.
I. Harvard business review.   II. Series: Harvard business review paperback series.
HD62.5.H3738  1999
658.4'21—dc21                        98-31399
                                     CIP

*The paper used in this publication meets the requirements of the American National Standard for Permanence of Paper for Printed Library Materials Z39.49-1984.*

# Contents

# The Questions Every Entrepreneur Must Answer

AMAR BHIDE

## Executive Summary

DIVERSIFY YOUR PRODUCT LINE. Stick to your knitting.
Hire a professional manager. Watch fixed costs. Those
are some of the suggestions that entrepreneurs sort
through as they try to get their ventures off the ground.
Why all the conflicting advice? Because in a young
company, all decisions are up for grabs.

Based on his observations of several hundred start-up
ventures over eight years, Amar Bhide has developed a
three-step sequence of questions that all entrepreneurs
must ask themselves in order to establish priorities
among the vast array of opportunities and problems
they face: What are my goals? Do I have the right strategy? Can I execute the strategy?

Before entrepreneurs can set goals for a business,
they must articulate their personal goals. They may want,
for instance, to attain a certain lifestyle, experiment with

technology, or build an institution that can outlive them. Only when entrepreneurs decide what they want from their businesses can they determine what kind of company they must build, what they are willing to risk, and whether they have a well-defined strategy.

Great strategies, however, don't guarantee great execution. A venture may fail if its founders do not hire the best people, attract capital, invest in organizational infrastructure, and shape a culture to suit the venture's strategy.

Founders must also consider the evolution of their personal roles. Entrepreneurs cannot build self-sustaining companies simply by "letting go." While they sketch out the future, entrepreneurs must manage as if the company were about to go under. They must continually acquire new skills—and continually ask themselves where they want to go and how they will get there.

---

OF THE HUNDREDS OF THOUSANDS OF BUSINESS VENTURES that entrepreneurs launch every year, many never get off the ground. Others fizzle after spectacular rocket starts.

A six-year-old condiment company has attracted loyal customers but has achieved less than $500,000 in sales. The company's gross margins can't cover its overhead or provide adequate incomes for the founder and the family members who participate in the business. Additional growth will require a huge capital infusion, but investors and potential buyers aren't keen on small, marginally profitable ventures, and the family has exhausted its resources.

Another young company, profitable and growing rapidly, imports novelty products from the Far East and sells them to large U.S. chain stores. The founder, who has a paper net worth of several million dollars, has been nominated for entrepreneur-of-the-year awards. But the company's spectacular growth has forced him to reinvest most of his profits to finance the business's growing inventories and receivables. Furthermore, the company's profitability has attracted competitors and tempted customers to deal directly with the Asian suppliers. If the founder doesn't do something soon, the business will evaporate.

Like most entrepreneurs, the condiment maker and the novelty importer get plenty of confusing counsel: Diversify your product line. Stick to your knitting. Raise capital by selling equity. Don't risk losing control just because things are bad. Delegate. Act decisively. Hire a professional manager. Watch your fixed costs.

*The problems entrepreneurs confront every day would overwhelm most managers.*

Why all the conflicting advice? Because the range of options—and problems—that founders of young businesses confront is vast. The manager of a mature company might ask, What business are we in? or How can we exploit our core competencies? Entrepreneurs must continually ask themselves what business they *want* to be in and what capabilities they would *like* to develop. Similarly, the organizational weaknesses and imperfections that entrepreneurs confront every day would cause the managers of a mature company to panic. Many young enterprises simultaneously lack coherent strategies, competitive strengths, talented employees, adequate controls, and clear reporting relationships.

The entrepreneur can tackle only one or two opportunities and problems at a time. Therefore, just as a parent should focus more on a toddler's motor skills than on his or her social skills, the entrepreneur must distinguish critical issues from normal growing pains.

Entrepreneurs cannot expect the sort of guidance and comfort that an authoritative child-rearing book can offer parents. Human beings pass through physiological and psychological stages in a more or less predetermined order, but companies do not share a developmental path. Microsoft, Lotus, WordPerfect, and Intuit, although competing in the same industry, did not evolve in the same way. Each of those companies has its own story to tell about the development of strategy and organizational structures and about the evolution of the founder's role in the enterprise.

*Every company has its own story to tell about the development of systems and strategy.*

The options that are appropriate for one entrepreneurial venture may be completely inappropriate for another. Entrepreneurs must make a bewildering number of decisions, and they must make the decisions that are right for them. The framework I present here and the accompanying rules of thumb will help entrepreneurs analyze the situations in which they find themselves, establish priorities among the opportunities and problems they face, and make rational decisions about the future. This framework, which is based on my observation of several hundred start-up ventures over eight years, doesn't prescribe answers. Instead, it helps entrepreneurs pose useful questions, identify important issues, and evaluate solutions. The framework applies whether the enterprise is a small printing shop trying to stay in business or a catalog retailer seeking hundreds of millions of dollars in sales. And it works at almost any point in a venture's evolution. Entrepreneurs should use the framework to evaluate their companies' position and trajectory often—not just when problems appear.

The framework consists of a three-step sequence of questions. The first step clarifies entrepreneurs' current goals, the second evaluates their strategies for attaining those goals, and the third helps them assess their capacity to execute their strategies. The hierarchical organization of the questions requires entrepreneurs to confront the basic, big-picture issues before they think about refinements and details. (See the exhibit "An Entre-

## An Entrepreneur's Guide to the Big Issues

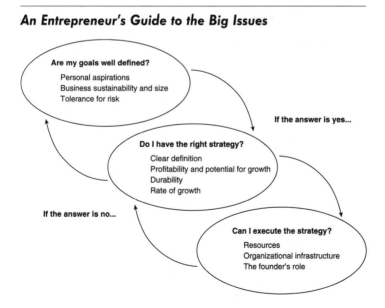

preneur's Guide to the Big Issues.") This approach does not assume that all companies—or all entrepreneurs—develop in the same way, so it does not prescribe a one-size-fits-all methodology for success.

## Clarifying Goals: Where Do I Want to Go?

An entrepreneur's personal and business goals are inextricably linked. Whereas the manager of a public company has a fiduciary responsibility to maximize value for shareholders, entrepreneurs build their businesses to fulfill personal goals and, if necessary, seek investors with similar goals.

Before they can set goals for a business, entrepreneurs must be explicit about their personal goals. And they must periodically ask themselves if those goals have changed. Many entrepreneurs say that they are launching their businesses to achieve independence and control their destiny, but those goals are too vague. If they stop and think about it, most entrepreneurs can identify goals that are more specific. For example, they may want an outlet for artistic talent, a chance to experiment with new technology, a flexible lifestyle, the rush that comes from rapid growth, or the immortality of building an institution that embodies their deeply held values. Financially, some entrepreneurs are looking for quick profits, some want to generate a satisfactory cash flow, and others seek capital gains from building and selling a company. Some entrepreneurs who want to build sustainable institutions do not consider personal financial returns a high priority. They may refuse acquisition proposals regardless of the price or sell equity cheaply to employees to secure their loyalty to the institution.

Only when entrepreneurs can say what they want personally from their businesses does it make sense for them to ask the following three questions:

## WHAT KIND OF ENTERPRISE DO I NEED TO BUILD?

Long-term sustainability does not concern entrepreneurs looking for quick profits from in-and-out deals. Similarly, so-called lifestyle entrepreneurs, who are interested only in generating enough of a cash flow to maintain a certain way of life, do not need to build businesses that could survive without them. But sustainability—or the perception thereof—matters greatly to entrepreneurs who hope to sell their businesses eventually. Sustainability is even more important for entrepreneurs who want to build an institution that is capable of renewing itself through changing generations of technology, employees, and customers.

Entrepreneurs' personal goals should also determine the target size of the businesses they launch. A lifestyle entrepreneur's venture needn't grow very large. In fact, a business that becomes too big might prevent the founder from enjoying life or remaining personally involved in all aspects of the work. In contrast, entrepreneurs seeking capital gains must build companies large enough to support an infrastructure that will not require their day-to-day intervention.

## WHAT RISKS AND SACRIFICES DOES SUCH AN ENTERPRISE DEMAND?

Building a sustainable business—that is, one whose principal productive asset is not just the founder's skills, contacts, and efforts—often entails making risky long-term bets. Unlike a solo consulting practice—which generates cash from the start—durable ventures, such as companies that produce branded consumer goods, need continued investment to build sustainable advantages. For instance, entrepreneurs may have to advertise to build a brand name. To pay for ad campaigns, they may have to reinvest profits, accept equity partners, or personally guarantee debt. To build depth in their organizations, entrepreneurs may have to trust inexperienced employees to make crucial decisions. Furthermore, many years may pass before any payoff materializes—if it materializes at all. Sustained risk-taking can be stressful. As one entrepreneur observes, "When you start, you just do it, like the Nike ad says. You are naïve because you haven't made your mistakes yet. Then you learn about all the things that can go wrong. And because your equity now has value, you feel you have a lot more to lose."

Entrepreneurs who operate small-scale, or lifestyle, ventures face different risks and stresses. Talented people usually avoid companies that offer no stock options and only limited opportunities for personal growth, so the entrepreneur's long hours may never end. Because personal franchises are difficult to sell

*To set meaningful goals, entrepreneurs must reconcile what they want with what they are willing to risk.*

and often require the owner's daily presence, founders may become locked into their businesses. They may face financial distress if they become sick or just burn out. "I'm always running, running, running," complains one entrepreneur, whose business earns him half a million dollars per year. "I work 14-hour days, and I can't remember the last time I took a vacation. I would like to sell the business, but who wants to buy a company with no infrastructure or employees?"

## CAN I ACCEPT THOSE RISKS AND SACRIFICES?

Entrepreneurs must reconcile what they want with what they are willing to risk. Consider Joseph Alsop, cofounder and president of Progress Software Corporation. When Alsop launched the company in 1981, he was in his mid-thirties, with a wife and three children. With that responsibility, he says, he didn't want to take the risks necessary to build a multibillion-dollar corporation like Microsoft, but he and his partners were willing to assume the risks required to build something more than a personal service business. Consequently, they picked a market niche that was large enough to let them build a sustainable company but not so large that it would attract the industry's giants. They worked for two years without salaries and invested their personal savings. In ten years, they had built Progress into a $200 million publicly held company.

Entrepreneurs would do well to follow Alsop's example by thinking explicitly about what they are and are not willing to risk. If entrepreneurs find that their businesses—even if very successful—won't satisfy them personally, or if they discover that achieving their personal goals requires them to take more risks and make more sacrifices than they are willing to, they need to reset their goals. When entrepreneurs have aligned their personal and their business goals, they must then make sure that they have the right strategy.

# Setting Strategy: How Will I Get There?

Many entrepreneurs start businesses to seize short-term opportunities without thinking about long-term strategy. Successful entrepreneurs, however, soon make the transition from a tactical to a strategic orientation so that they can begin to build crucial capabilities and resources.

Formulating a sound strategy is more basic to a young company than resolving hiring issues, designing control systems, setting reporting relationships, or defining the founder's role. Ventures based on a good strategy can survive confusion and poor leadership, but sophisticated control systems and organizational structures cannot compensate for an unsound strategy. Entrepreneurs should periodically put their strategies to the following four tests:

## IS THE STRATEGY WELL DEFINED?

A company's strategy will fail all other tests if it doesn't provide a clear direction for the enterprise. Even solo entrepreneurs can benefit from a defined strategy. For example, deal makers who specialize in particular industries or types of transactions often have better access to potential deals than generalists do. Similarly, independent consultants can charge higher fees if they have a reputation for expertise in a particular area.

An entrepreneur who wants to build a sustainable company must formulate a bolder and more explicit strategy. The strategy should integrate the entrepreneur's aspirations with specific long-term policies about the needs the company will serve, its geographic reach, its technological capabilities, and other strategic considerations. To help attract people and resources, the strategy must embody the entrepreneur's vision of where the company is going instead of where it is. The strategy must also provide a framework for making the decisions and setting the policies that will take the company there.

The strategy articulated by the founders of Sun Microsystems, for instance, helped them make smart decisions as they developed the company. From the outset, they decided that Sun would forgo the niche-market strategy commonly used by Silicon Valley start-ups. Instead, they elected to compete with industry leaders IBM and Digital by building and marketing a general-purpose workstation. That strategy, recalls cofounder and former president Vinod Khosla, made Sun's product-development choices obvious. "We wouldn't develop any applications software," he explains. This strategy also dictated that Sun assume the risk of building a direct sales force and providing its own field support—just like its much larger competitors. "The Moon or Bust was our motto," Khosla says. The founders' bold vision helped attract premier venture-capital firms and gave Sun extraordinary visibility within its industry.

*A new company's strategy must embody the founder's vision of where the company is going, not where it is.*

To be useful, strategy statements should be concise and easily understood by key constituents such as employees, investors, and customers. They must also preclude activities and investments that, although they seem attractive, would deplete the company's resources.

A strategy that is so broadly stated that it permits a company to do anything is tantamount to no strategy at all. For instance, claiming to be in the leisure and entertainment business does not preclude a tent manufacturer from operating casinos or making films. Defining the venture as a high-performance outdoor-gear company provides a much more useful focus.

## CAN THE STRATEGY GENERATE SUFFICIENT PROFITS AND GROWTH?

Once entrepreneurs have formulated clear strategies, they must determine whether those strategies will allow the ventures to be profitable and to grow to a desirable size. The failure to earn satisfactory returns should prompt entrepreneurs to ask tough questions: What's the source, if any, of our competitive edge? Are our offerings really better than our competitors'? If they are, does the premium we can charge justify the additional costs we incur, and can we move enough volume at higher prices to cover our fixed costs? If we are in a commodity business, are our costs lower than our competitors'? Disappointing growth should also raise concerns: Is the market large enough? Do diseconomies of scale make profitable growth impossible?

No amount of hard work can turn a kitten into a lion. When a new venture is faltering, entrepreneurs must address basic economic issues. For instance, many people are attracted to personal service businesses, such as laundries and tax-preparation services, because they can start and operate those businesses just by working hard. They don't have to worry about confronting large competitors, raising a lot of capital, or developing proprietary technology. But the factors that make it easy for entrepreneurs to launch such businesses often prevent them from attaining their long-term goals. Businesses based on an entrepreneur's willingness to work hard usually confront other equally determined competitors. Furthermore, it is difficult to make such companies large enough to support employees and infrastructure. Besides, if employees can do what the founder does, they have little incentive to stay with the venture. Founders of such companies often cannot have the lifestyle they want, no matter how talented they are. With no way to leverage their skills, they can eat only what they kill.

Entrepreneurs who are stuck in ventures that are unprofitable and cannot grow satisfactorily must take radical action. They must find a new industry or develop innovative economies of scale or scope in their existing fields. Rebecca Matthias, for example, started Mothers Work in 1982 to sell maternity clothing to professional women by mail order. Mail-order businesses are easy to start, but with tens of thousands of catalogs vying for consumers' attention, low response rates usually lead to low profitability—a reality that Matthias confronted after three years in the business. In 1985, she borrowed $150,000 to open the first retail store specializing in maternity clothes for working women. By 1994, Mothers Work was operating 175 stores generating about $59 million in revenues.

One alternative to radical action is to stick with the failing venture and hope for the big order that's just around the corner or the greater fool who will buy the business. Both hopes are usually futile. It's best to walk away.

## IS THE STRATEGY SUSTAINABLE?

The next issue entrepreneurs must confront is whether their strategies can serve the enterprise over the long term. The issue of sustainability is especially significant for entrepreneurs who have been riding the wave of a new technology, a regulatory change, or any other change—exogenous to the business—that creates situations in which supply cannot keep up with demand. Entrepreneurs who catch a wave can prosper at the outset just because the trend is on their side; they are competing not with one another but with outmoded players. But what happens when the wave crests? As market imbalances disappear, so do many of the erstwhile high fliers who had never developed distinctive capabilities or established defensible competitive positions. Wave riders must anticipate market saturation, intensifying competition, and the next wave. They have to abandon the me-too approach in favor of a new, more durable business model. Or they may be able to sell their high-growth businesses for handsome prices in spite of the dubious long-term prospects.

Consider Edward Rosen, who cofounded Vydec in 1972. The company developed one of the first stand-alone word processors, and as the market for the machines exploded, Vydec rocketed to $90 million in revenues in its sixth year, with nearly 1,000 employees in the United States and Europe. But Rosen and his partner could see that the days of stand-alone word processors were numbered. They happily accepted an offer from Exxon to buy the company for more than $100 million.

Such forward thinking is an exception. Entrepreneurs in rapidly growing companies often don't consider exit strategies seriously. Encouraged by short-term success, they continue to reinvest profits in unsustainable businesses until all they have left is memories of better days.

Entrepreneurs who start ventures not by catching a wave but by creating their own wave face a different set of challenges in crafting a sustainable strategy. They must build on their initial strength by developing multiple strengths. Brand-new ventures usually cannot afford to innovate on every front. Few start-ups, for example, can expect to attract the resources needed to market a revolutionary product that requires radical advances in technology, a new manufacturing process, and new distribution channels. Cash-strapped entrepreneurs usually focus first on building and exploiting a few sources of uniqueness and use standard, readily available elements in the rest of the business. Michael Dell, the founder of Dell Computer, for example, made low price an option for personal computer buyers by assembling standard components in a college dormitory room and selling by mail order without frills or much sales support.

*It's easy to knock off an innovative product, but an innovative business system is much harder to replicate.*

Strategies for taking the hill, however, won't necessarily hold it. A model based on one or two strengths becomes obsolete as success begets imitation. For instance, competitors can easily knock off an entrepreneur's innovative product. But they will find it much more difficult to replicate *systems* that incorporate many distinct and complementary capabilities. A business with an attractive product line, well-integrated manufacturing and logistics, close relationships with distributors, a culture of responsiveness to customers, and the capability to produce a continuing stream of product innovations is not easy to copy.

Entrepreneurs who build desirable franchises must quickly find ways to broaden their competitive capabilities. For example, software start-up Intuit's first product, Quicken, had more attractive features and was easier to use than other personal-finance software programs. Intuit realized, however, that competitors could also make their products easy to use, so the company took advantage of its early lead to invest in a variety of strengths. Intuit enhanced its position with distributors by introducing a family of products for small businesses, including QuickBooks, an accounting program. It brought sophisticated marketing techniques to an industry that "viewed customer calls as interruptions to the sacred art of programming," according to the company's founder and chairman, Scott Cook. It established a superior product-design process with multifunctional teams that included marketing and technical support. And Intuit invested heavily to provide customers with outstanding technical support for free.

## ARE MY GOALS FOR GROWTH TOO CONSERVATIVE OR TOO AGGRESSIVE?

After defining or redefining the business and verifying its basic soundness, an entrepreneur should determine whether plans for its growth are appropriate. Different enterprises can and should grow at different rates. Setting the right pace is as important to a young business as it is to a novice bicyclist. For either one, too fast or too slow can lead to a fall. The optimal growth rate for a fledgling enterprise is a function of many interdependent factors. (See "Finding the Right Growth Rate" on page 24.)

# Executing the Strategy: Can I Do It?

The third question entrepreneurs must ask themselves may be the hardest to answer because it requires the most candid self-examination: Can I execute the strategy? Great ideas don't guarantee great performance. Many young companies fail because the entrepreneur can't execute the strategy; for instance, the venture may run out of cash, or the entrepreneur may be unable to generate sales or fill orders. Entrepreneurs must examine three areas—resources, organizational capabilities, and their personal roles—to evaluate their ability to carry out their strategies.

## DO I HAVE THE RIGHT RESOURCES AND RELATIONSHIPS?

The lack of talented employees is often the first obstacle to the successful implementation of a strategy. During the start-up phase, many ventures cannot attract top-notch employees, so the founders perform most of the crucial tasks themselves and recruit whomever they can to help out. After that initial period, entrepreneurs can and should be ambitious in seeking new talent, especially if they want their businesses to grow quickly.

*Entrepreneurs who hope to turn underqualified employees into star performers are almost always disappointed.*

Entrepreneurs who hope that they can turn underqualified and inexperienced employees into star performers eventually reach the conclusion, along with Intuit founder Cook, that "you can't coach height." Moreover, after a venture establishes even a short track record, it can attract a much higher caliber of employee.

In determining how to upgrade the workforce, entrepreneurs must address many complex and sensitive issues: Should I recruit individuals for specific slots or, as is commonly the case in talent-starved organizations, should I create positions for promising candidates? Are the recruits going to manage or replace existing employees? How extensive should the replacements be? Should the replacement process be gradual or quick? Should I, with my personal attachment to the business, make termination decisions myself or should I bring in outsiders?

A young venture needs more than internal resources. Entrepreneurs must also consider their customers and sources of capital. Ventures often start with the customers they can attract the most quickly, which may not be the customers the company eventually needs. Similarly, entrepreneurs who begin by bootstrapping, using money from friends and family or loans from local banks, must often find richer sources of capital to build sustainable businesses.

For a new venture to survive, some resources that initially are external may have to become internal. Many start-ups operate at first as virtual enterprises because the founders cannot afford to produce in-house and hire employees, and because they value flexibility. But the flexibility that comes from owning few resources is a double-edged sword. Just as a young company is free to stop placing orders, suppliers can stop filling them. Furthermore, a company with no assets signals to customers and potential investors that the entrepreneur may not be committed for the long haul. A business with no employees and hard assets may also be difficult to sell, because potential buyers will probably worry that the company will vanish when the founder departs. To build a durable company, an entrepreneur may have to consider integrating vertically or replacing subcontractors with full-time employees.

## HOW STRONG IS THE ORGANIZATION?

An organization's capacity to execute its strategy depends on its "hard" infrastructure—its organizational structure and systems—and on its "soft" infrastruture—its culture and norms.

The hard infrastructure an entrepreneurial company needs depends on its goals and strategies. (See "Investing in Organizational Infrastructure" on page 26.) Some entrepreneurs want to build geographically dispersed businesses, realize synergies by sharing resources across business units, establish first-mover advantages through rapid growth, and eventually go public. They must invest more in organizational infrastructure than their couterparts who want to build simple, single-location businesses at a cautious pace.

A venture's growth rate provides an important clue to whether the entrepreneur has invested too much or too little in the company's structure and systems. If performance is sluggish—if, for example, growth lags behind expectations and new products are late—excessive rules and controls may be stifling employees. If, in contrast, the business is growing rapidly and gaining share, inadequate reporting mechanisms and controls are a more likely concern. When a new venture is growing at a fast pace, entrepreneurs must simultaneously give new employees considerable responsibility and monitor their finances very closely. Companies like Blockbuster Video cope by giving frontline employees all the operating autonomy they can handle while maintaining tight, centralized financial controls.

An evolving organization's culture also has a profound influence on how well it can execute its strategy. Culture determines the personalities and temperaments of the workforce; lone wolves are unlikely to want to work in a consensual organization, whereas shy introverts may avoid rowdy outfits. Culture fills in the gaps that an organization's written rules do not anticipate. Culture determines the degree to which individual employees and organizational units compete and cooperate, and how they treat customers. More than any other factor, culture determines whether an organization can cope with the crises and discontinuities of growth.

Unlike organizational structures and systems, which entrepreneurs often copy from other companies, culture must be custom built. As many software makers have found, for instance, a laid-back organization can't compete well against Microsoft. The rambunctiousness of a start-up trading operation may scare away the conservative clients the venture wants to attract. A

*When entrepreneurs don't stop to think about culture, their companies develop one by chance rather than by design.*

culture that fits a company's strategy, however, can lead to spectacular performance. Physician Sales & Service (PSS), a medical-products distribution company, has grown from $13 million in sales in 1987 to nearly $500 million in 1995, from 5 branches in Florida to 56 branches covering every state in the continental United States, and from 120 employees to 1,800. Like other rapidly growing companies, PSS has tight financial controls. But, venture capitalist Thomas Dickerson says, "PSS would be just another efficiently managed distribution company if it didn't have a corporate culture that is obsessed with meeting customers' needs and maintaining a meritocracy. PSS employees are motivated by the culture to provide unmatched customer service."

When entrepreneurs neglect to articulate organizational norms and instead hire employees mainly for their technical skills and credentials, their organizations develop a culture by chance rather than by design. The personalities and values of the first wave of employees shape a culture that may not serve the founders' goals and strategies. Once a culture is established, it is difficult to change.

### CAN I PLAY MY ROLE?

Entrepreneurs who aspire to operate small enterprises in which they perform all crucial tasks never have to change their roles. In personal service companies, for instance, the founding partners often perform client work from the time they start the company until they retire. Transforming a fledgling enterprise into an entity capable of an independent existence, however, requires founders to undertake new roles.

Founders cannot build self-sustaining organizations simply by "letting go." Before entrepreneurs have the option of doing less, they first must do much more. If the business model is not sustainable, they must create a new one. To secure the resources demanded by an ambitious strategy, they must manage the perceptions of the resource providers: potential customers, employees, and investors. To build an enterprise that will be able to function without them, entrepreneurs must design the organization's structure and systems and mold its culture and character.

While they are sketching out an expansive view of the future, entrepreneurs also have to manage as if the company were on the verge of going under, keeping a firm grip on expenses and monitoring performance. They have to inspire and coach employees while dealing with the unpleasantness of firing those who will not be able to grow with the company. Bill Nussey, cofounder of the software maker Da Vinci Systems Corporation, recalls that firing employees who had "struggled and cried and sacrificed with the company" was the hardest thing he ever had to do.

Few successful entrepreneurs ever come to play a purely visionary role in their organizations. They remain deeply engaged in what Abraham Zaleznik, the Konosuke Matsushita Professor of Leadership Emeritus at the Harvard Business School, calls the "real work" of their enterprises. Marvin Bower, the founding partner of McKinsey & Company, continued to negotiate and direct studies for clients while leading the firm through a considerable expansion of its size and geographic reach. Bill Gates, cofounder and CEO of multibillion-dollar software powerhouse Microsoft, reportedly still reviews the code that programmers write.

But founders' roles must change. Gates no longer *writes* programs. Michael Roberts, an expert on entrepreneurship, suggests that an entrepreneur's role should evolve from doing the work, to teaching others how to do it, to prescribing desired results, and eventually to managing the overall context in which the work is done. One entrepreneur speaks of changing from quarterback to coach. Whatever the metaphor, the idea is that leaders seek ever increasing impact from what they do. They achieve this by, for example, focusing more on formulating marketing strategies than on selling; negotiating and reviewing budgets rather than directly supervising work;

designing incentive plans rather than setting the compensation of individual employees; negotiating the acquisitions of companies instead of the cost of office supplies; and developing a common purpose and organizational norms rather than moving a product out the door.

In evaluating their personal roles, therefore, entrepreneurs should ask themselves whether they continually experiment with new jobs and responsibilities. Founders who simply spend more hours performing the same tasks and making the same decisions as the business grows end up hindering growth. They should ask themselves whether they have acquired any new skills recently. An entrepreneur who is an engineer, for example, might master financial analysis. If founders can't point to new skills, they are probably in a rut and their roles aren't evolving.

Entrepreneurs must ask themselves whether they actually want to change and learn. People who enjoy taking on new challenges and acquiring new skills—Bill Gates, again—can lead a venture from the start-up stage to market dominance. But some people, such as H. Wayne Huizenga, the moving spirit behind Waste Management and Blockbuster Video, are much happier moving on to get other ventures off the ground. Entrepreneurs have a responsibility to themselves and to the people who depend on them to understand what fulfills and frustrates them personally.

Many great enterprises spring from modest, improvised beginnings. William Hewlett and David Packard tried to craft a bowling alley foot-fault indicator and a harmonica tuner before developing their first successful product, an audio oscillator. Wal-Mart Stores' founder, Sam Walton, started by buying what he called a "real dog" of a franchised variety store in Newport, Arkansas, because his wife wanted to live in a small town. Speedy response and trial and error were more important to those companies at the start-up stage than foresight and planning. But pure improvisation—or luck—rarely yields long-term success. Hewlett-Packard might still be an obscure outfit if its founders had not eventually made conscious decisions about product lines, technological capabilities, debt policies, and organizational norms.

Entrepreneurs, with their powerful bias for action, often avoid thinking about the big issues of goals, strategies, and capabilities. They must, sooner or later, consciously structure such inquiry into their companies and their lives. Lasting success requires entrepreneurs to keep asking tough questions about where they want to go and whether the track they are on will take them there.

## Finding the Right Growth Rate

FINDING THE OPTIMAL GROWTH RATE for a new enterprise is a difficult and critical task. To set the right pace, entrepreneurs must consider many factors, including the following:

### Economies of scale, scope, or customer network

The greater the returns to a company's scale, scope, or the size of its customer network, the stronger the case for pursuing rapid growth. When scale causes profitability to increase considerably, growth soon pays for itself. And in industries in which economies of scale or scope limit the number of viable competitors, establishing a favorable economic position first can help deter rivals.

## The ability to lock in customers or scarce resources

Rapid growth also makes sense if consumers are inclined to stick with the companies with which they initially do business, either because of an aversion to change or because of the expense of switching to another company. Similarly, in retail, growing rapidly can allow a company to secure the most favorable locations or dominate a geographic area that can support only one large store, even if national economies of scale are limited.

## Competitors' growth

If rivals are expanding quickly, a company may be forced to do the same. In markets in which one company generally sets the industry's standard, such as the market for personal-computer operating-system software, growing quickly enough to stay ahead of the pack may be a young company's only hope.

## Resource constraints

A new venture will not be able to grow rapidly if there is a shortage of skilled employees or if investors and lenders are unwilling to fund an expansion that they consider reckless. A venture that is growing quickly, however, will be able to attract capital as well as the employees and customers who want to go with a winner.

## Internal financing capability

When a new venture is not able to attract investors or borrow at reasonable terms, its internal financing capability will determine the pace at which it can grow. Businesses that have high profit margins and low assets-to-sales ratios can fund high growth rates. A self-funded business, according to the well-known sustainable growth formula, cannot expand its revenues at a rate faster than its return on equity.

### Tolerant customers

When a company is young and growing rapidly, its products and services often contain some flaws. In some markets, such as certain segments of the high-tech industry, customers are accustomed to imperfect offerings and may even derive some pleasure from complaining about them. Companies in such markets can expand quickly. But in markets in which buyers will not stand for breakdowns and bugs, such as the market for luxury goods and mission-critical process-control systems, growth should be much more cautious.

### Personal temperament and goals

Some entrepreneurs thrive on rapid growth; others are uncomfortable with the crises and fire fighting that usually accompany it. One of the limits on a new venture's growth should be the entrepreneur's tolerance for stress and discomfort.

## Investing in Organizational Infrastructure

FEW ENTREPRENEURS START OUT WITH BOTH a well-defined strategy and a plan for developing an organization that can achieve that strategy. In fact, many start-ups, which don't have formal control systems, decision-making processes, or clear roles for employees, can hardly be called organizations. The founders of such ventures improvise. They perform most of the important functions themselves and make decisions as they go along.

Informality is fine as long as entrepreneurs aren't interested in building a large, sustainable business. Once that becomes their goal, however, they must start developing formal systems and processes. Such organizational infrastructure allows a venture to grow, but at the same time, it increases overhead and may slow down decisionmaking. How much infrastructure is enough and how much is too much? To match investments in infrastructure to the requirements of a venture's strategy, entrepreneurs must consider the degree to which their strategy depends on the following:

**Delegating tasks**

As a young venture grows, its founders will probably need to delegate many of the tasks that they used to perform. To get employees to perform those tasks competently and diligently, the founders may need to establish mechanisms to monitor employees and standard operating procedures and policies. Consider an extreme example. Randy and Debbi Fields pass along their skills and knowledge through software that tells employees in every Mrs. Fields Cookies shop exactly how to make cookies and operate the business. The software analyzes data such as local weather conditions and the day of the week to generate hourly instructions about such matters as which cookies to bake, when to offer free samples, and when to reorder chocolate chips.

Telling employees how to do their jobs, however, can stifle initiative. Companies that require frontline employees to act quickly and resourcefully might decide to focus more on outcomes than on behavior, using control systems that set performance targets for employees, compare results against objectives, and provide appropriate incentives.

## Specializing tasks

In a small-scale start-up, everyone does a little bit of everything, but as a business grows and tries to achieve economies of scale and scope, employees must be assigned clearly defined roles and grouped into appropriate organizational units. An all-purpose workshop employee, for example, might become a machine tool operator, who is part of a manufacturing unit. Specialized activities need to be integrated by, for example, creating the position of a general manager, who coordinates the manufacturing and marketing functions, or through systems that are designed to measure and reward employees for cross-functional cooperation. Poor integrative mechanisms are why geographic expansion, vertical integration, broadening of product lines, and other strategies to achieve economies of scale and scope often fail.

## Mobilizing funds for growth

Cash-strapped businesses that are trying to grow need good systems to forecast and monitor the availability of funds. Outside sources of capital such as banks often refuse to advance funds to companies with weak controls and organizational infrastructure.

## Creating a track record

If entrepreneurs hope to build a company that they can sell, they must start preparing early. Public markets and potential acquirers like to see an extended history of well-kept financial records and controls to reassure them of the soundness of the business.

**Originally published in November–December 1996
Reprint 96603**

# How to Write a Great Business Plan

WILLIAM A. SAHLMAN

## Executive Summary

EVERY SEASONED INVESTOR knows that detailed financial projections for a new company are an act of imagination. Nevertheless, most business plans pour far too much ink on the numbers—and far too little on the information that really matters. Why? William Sahlman suggests that a great business plan is one that focuses on a series of questions. These questions relate to the four factors critical to the success of every new venture: the people, the opportunity, the context, and the possibilities for both risk and reward.

The questions about people revolve around three issues: What do they know? Whom do they know? and How well are they known? As for opportunity, the plan should focus on two questions: Is the market for the venture's product or service large or rapidly growing (or preferably both)? and Is the industry structurally attractive? Then, in addition to demonstrating an understanding of the context in which their venture will operate, entrepreneurs should make clear how they will respond when that context inevitably changes. Finally, the plan should look unflinchingly at the risks the new venture faces, giving would-be backers a realistic idea of what magnitude of reward they can expect and when they can expect it.

A great business plan is not easy to compose, Sahlman acknowledges, largely because most entrepreneurs are wild-eyed optimists. But one that asks the right questions is a powerful tool. A better deal, not to mention a better shot at success, awaits entrepreneurs who use it.

---

F EW AREAS OF BUSINESS ATTRACT as much attention as new ventures, and few aspects of new-venture creation attract as much attention as the business plan. Countless books and articles in the popular press dissect the topic. A growing number of annual business-plan contests are springing up across the United States and, increasingly, in other countries. Both graduate and undergraduate schools devote entire courses to the subject. Indeed, judging by all the hoopla surrounding business plans, you would think that the only things standing between a would-be entrepreneur and spectacular success are glossy five-color charts, a bundle of meticulous-looking spreadsheets, and a decade of month-by-month financial projections.

Nothing could be further from the truth. In my experience with hundreds of entrepreneurial start-ups, business plans rank no higher than 2—on a scale from 1 to

10—as a predictor of a new venture's success. (See "Business Plans: For Entrepreneurs Only?" on page 49.) And sometimes, in fact, the more elaborately crafted the document, the more likely the venture is to, well, flop, for lack of a more euphemistic word.

What's wrong with most business plans? The answer is relatively straightforward. Most waste too much ink on numbers and devote too little to the information that really matters to intelligent investors. As every seasoned investor knows, financial projections for a new company—especially detailed, month-by-month projections that stretch out for more than a year—are an act of imagination. An entrepreneurial venture faces far too many unknowns to predict revenues, let alone profits. Moreover, few if any entrepreneurs correctly anticipate how much capital and time will be required to accomplish their objectives. Typically, they are wildly optimistic, padding their projections. Investors know about the padding effect and therefore discount the figures in business plans. These maneuvers create a vicious circle of inaccuracy that benefits no one. (See "A Glossary of Business Plan Terms" on page 51.)

Don't misunderstand me: business plans should include some numbers. But those numbers should appear mainly in the form of a business model that shows the entrepreneurial team has thought through the key drivers of the venture's success or failure. In manufacturing, such a driver might be the yield on a production process; in magazine publishing, the anticipated renewal rate; or in software, the impact of using various distribution channels. The model should also address the break-even issue: At what level of sales does the business begin to make a profit? And even more important, When does cash flow turn positive? Without a doubt, these questions deserve a few pages in any business plan. Near the back.

What goes at the front? What information does a good business plan contain?

If you want to speak the language of investors—and also make sure you have asked yourself the right questions before setting out on the most daunting journey of a businessperson's career—I recommend basing your business plan on the framework that follows. It does not provide the kind of "winning" formula touted by some current how-to books and software programs for entrepreneurs. Nor is it a guide to brain surgery. Rather, the framework systematically assesses the four interdependent factors critical to every new venture:

**The People.**  The men and women starting and running the venture, as well as the outside parties providing key services or important resources for it, such as its lawyers, accountants, and suppliers.

**The Opportunity.**  A profile of the business itself—what it will sell and to whom, whether the business can grow and how fast, what its economics are, who and what stand in the way of success.

**The Context.**  The big picture—the regulatory environment, interest rates, demographic trends, inflation, and the like—basically, factors that inevitably change but cannot be controlled by the entrepreneur.

**Risk and Reward.**  An assessment of everything that can go wrong and right, and a discussion of how the entrepreneurial team can respond.

The assumption behind the framework is that great businesses have attributes that are easy to identify but hard to assemble. They have an experienced, energetic managerial team from the top to the bottom. The team's members have skills and experiences directly relevant to the opportunity they are pursuing. Ideally, they will have worked successfully together in the past. The opportunity has an attractive, sustainable business model; it is possible to create a competitive edge and defend it. Many options exist for expanding the scale and scope of the business, and these options are unique to the enterprise and its team. Value can be extracted from the business in a number of ways either through a positive harvest event—a sale—or by scaling down or liquidating. The context is favorable with respect to both the regulatory and the macro-economic environments. Risk is understood, and the team has considered ways to mitigate the impact of difficult events. In short, great businesses have the four parts of the framework completely covered. If only reality were so neat.

## The People

When I receive a business plan, I always read the résumé section first. Not because the people part of the new venture is the most important, but because without the right team, none of the other parts really matters.

I read the résumés of the venture's team with a list of questions in mind. (See "Who Are These People, Anyway?" on page 53.) All these questions get at the same three issues about the venture's team members: What do they know? Whom do they know? and How well are they known?

What and whom they know are matters of insight and experience. How familiar are the team members with industry players and dynamics? Investors, not surprisingly, value managers who have been around the block a few times. A business plan should candidly describe each team member's knowledge of the new venture's type of product or service; its production processes; and the market itself, from competitors to customers. It also helps to indicate whether the team members have worked together before. Not played—as in roomed together in college—but *worked.*

Investors also look favorably on a team that is known because the real world often prefers not to deal with start-ups. They're too unpredictable. That changes, however, when the new company is run by people well known to suppliers, customers, and employees. Their enterprise may be brand new, but they aren't. The surprise element of working with a start-up is somewhat ameliorated.

Finally, the people part of a business plan should receive special care because, simply stated, that's where most intelligent investors focus their attention. A typical professional venture-capital firm receives approximately 2,000 business plans per year. These plans are filled with tantalizing ideas for new products and services that will change the world and reap billions in the process—or so they say. But the fact is, most venture-capitalists believe that ideas are a dime a dozen: only execution skills count. As Arthur Rock, a venture capital legend associated with the formation of such companies as Apple, Intel, and Teledyne, states, "I invest in people, not ideas." Rock also has said, "If you can find good people, if they're wrong about the product, they'll make a switch, so what good is it to understand the product that they're talking about in the first place?"

Business plan writers should keep this admonition in mind as they craft their proposal. Talk about the people—exhaustively. And if there is nothing solid about their experience and abilities to herald, then the entrepreneurial team should think again about launching the venture.

## The Opportunity

When it comes to the opportunity itself, a good business plan begins by focusing on two questions: Is the total market for the venture's product or service large, rapidly growing, or both? Is the industry now, or can it become, structurally attractive? Entrepreneurs and investors look for large or rapidly growing markets mainly because it is often easier to obtain a share of a growing market than to fight with entrenched competitors for a share of a mature or stagnant market. Smart investors, in fact, try hard to identify high-growth-potential markets early in their evolution: that's where the big payoffs are. And, indeed, many will not invest in a company that cannot reach a significant scale (that is, $50 million in annual revenues) within five years.

As for attractiveness, investors are obviously looking for markets that actually allow businesses to make some money. But that's not the no-brainer it seems. In the late 1970s, the computer disk-drive business looked very attractive. The technology was new and exciting. Dozens of companies jumped into the fray, aided by an army of professional investors. Twenty years later, however, the thrill is gone for managers and investors alike. Disk drive companies must design products to meet the perceived needs of original equipment manufacturers (OEMs) and end users. Selling a product to OEMs is complicated. The customers are large relative to most of their suppliers. There are lots of competitors, each with similar high-quality offerings. Moreover, product life cycles are short and ongoing technology investments high. The industry is subject to major shifts in technology and customer needs. Intense rivalry leads to lower prices and, hence, lower margins. In short, the disk-drive industry is simply not set up to make people a lot of money; it's a structural disaster area.

The information services industry, by contrast, is paradise. Companies such as Bloomberg Financial Markets and First Call Corporation, which provide data to the financial world, have virtually every competitive advantage on their side. First, they can assemble or create *proprietary* content—content that, by the way, is like life's blood to thousands of money managers and stock analysts around the world. And although it is often expensive to develop the service and to acquire initial customers, once up and running, these companies can deliver content to customers very cheaply. Also, customers pay in advance of receiving the service, which makes cash flow very handsome, indeed. In short, the structure of the information services industry is beyond attractive: it's gorgeous. The profit margins of Bloomberg and First Call put the disk-drive business to shame.

Thus, the first step for entrepreneurs is to make sure they are entering an industry that is large and/or growing, and one that's structurally attractive. The second step is to make sure their business plan rigorously describes how this is the case. And if it isn't the case, their business plan needs to specify how the venture will still manage to make enough of a profit that investors (or potential employees or suppliers, for that matter) will want to participate.

Once it examines the new venture's industry, a business plan must describe in detail how the company will build and launch its product or service into the market-place. Again, a series of questions should guide the discussion. (See "The Opportunity of a Lifetime—or Is It?" on page 53.)

Often the answers to these questions reveal a fatal flaw in the business. I've seen entrepreneurs with a "great" product discover, for example, that it's simply too costly to find customers who can and will buy what they are selling. Economically viable access to customers is the key to business, yet many entrepreneurs

*The market is as fickle as it is unpredictable. Who would have guessed that plug-in room deodorizers would sell?*

take the *Field of Dreams* approach to this notion: build it, and they will come. That strategy works in the movies but is not very sensible in the real world.

It is not always easy to answer questions about the likely consumer response to new products or services. The market is as fickle as it is unpredictable. (Who would have guessed that plug-in room deodorizers would sell?) One entrepreneur I know proposed to introduce an electronic news-clipping service. He made his pitch to a prospective venture-capital investor who rejected the plan, stating, "I just don't think the dogs will eat the dog food." Later, when the entrepreneur's company went public, he sent the venture capitalist an anonymous package containing an empty can of dog food and a copy of his prospectus. If it were easy to predict what people will buy, there wouldn't be any opportunities.

Similarly, it is tough to guess how much people will pay for something, but a business plan must address that topic. Sometimes, the dogs will eat the dog food, but only at a price less than cost. Investors always look for opportunities for value pricing—that is, markets in which the costs to produce the product are low, but consumers will still pay a lot for it. No one is dying to invest in a company when margins are skinny. Still, there is money to be made in inexpensive products and service—even in commodities. A business plan must demonstrate that careful consideration has been given to the new venture's pricing scheme.

The list of questions about the new venture's opportunity focuses on the direct revenues and the costs of producing and marketing a product. That's fine, as far as it goes. A sensible proposal, however, also involves assessing the business model from a perspective that takes into account the investment required—that is, the balance sheet side of the equation. The following questions should also be addressed so that investors can understand the cash flow implications of pursuing an opportunity:

- When does the business have to buy resources, such as supplies, raw materials, and people?

- When does the business have to pay for them?

- How long does it take to acquire a customer?

- How long before the customer sends the business a check?

- How much capital equipment is required to support a dollar of sales?

Investors, of course, are looking for businesses in which management can buy low, sell high, collect early, and pay late. The business plan needs to spell out how close to that ideal the new venture is expected to come.

Even if the answer is "not very"—and it usually is—at least the truth is out there to discuss.

The opportunity section of a business plan must also bring a few other issues to the surface. First, it must demonstrate and analyze how an opportunity can grow—in other words, how the new venture can expand its range of products or services, customer base, or geographic scope. Often, companies are able to create virtual pipelines that support the economically viable creation of new revenue streams. In the publishing business, for example, *Inc.* magazine has expanded its product line to include seminars, books, and videos

*Whatever the reason, better-mousetrap businesses have an uncanny way of malfunctioning.*

about entrepreneurship. Similarly, building on the success of its personal-finance software program Quicken, Intuit now sells software for electronic banking, small-business accounting, and tax preparation, as well as personal-printing supplies and on-line information services—to name just a few of its highly profitable ancillary spin-offs.

Now, lots of business plans runneth over on the subject of the new venture's potential for growth and expansion. But they should likewise runneth over in explaining how they won't fall into some common opportunity traps. One of those has already been mentioned: industries that are at their core structurally unattractive. But there are others. The world of invention, for example, is fraught with danger. Over the past 15 years, I have seen scores of individuals who have devised a better mousetrap—newfangled creations from inflatable pillows for use on airplanes to automated car-parking systems. Few of these idea-driven companies have really taken off, however. I'm not entirely sure why. Sometimes, the inventor refuses to spend the money required by or share the rewards sufficiently with the business side of the company. Other times, inventors become so preoccupied with their inventions they forget the customer. Whatever the reason, better-mousetrap businesses have an uncanny way of malfunctioning.

Another opportunity trap that business plans—and entrepreneurs in general—need to pay attention to is the tricky business of arbitrage. Basically, arbitrage ventures are created to take advantage of some pricing disparity in the marketplace. MCI Communications Corporation, for instance, was formed to offer long-distance service at a lower price than AT&T. Some of the industry consolidations going on today reflect a different kind of arbitrage—the ability to buy small businesses at a wholesale price, roll them up together into a larger package, and take them public at a retail price, all without necessarily adding value in the process.

Taking advantage of arbitrage opportunities is a viable and potentially profitable way to enter a business. In the final analysis, however, all arbitrage opportunities evaporate. It is not a question of whether, only when. The trick in these businesses is to use the arbitrage profits to build a more enduring business model, and business plans must explain how and when that will occur.

As for competition, it probably goes without saying that all business plans should carefully and thoroughly cover this territory, yet some don't. That is a glaring omission. For starters, every business plan should answer the following questions about the competition:

- Who are the new venture's current competitors?

- What resources do they control? What are their strengths and weaknesses?

- How will they respond to the new venture's decision to enter the business?

- How can the new venture respond to its competitors' response?

- Who else might be able to observe and exploit the same opportunity?

- Are there ways to co-opt potential or actual competitors by forming alliances?

Business is like chess: to be successful, you must anticipate several moves in advance. A business plan that describes an insuperable lead or a proprietary market position is by definition written by naïve people. That goes not just for the competition section of the business plan but for the entire discussion of the opportunity. All opportunities have promise; all have vulnerabilities. A good business plan doesn't whitewash the latter. Rather, it proves that the entrepreneurial team knows the good, the bad, and the ugly that the venture faces ahead.

## The Context

Opportunities exist in a context. At one level is the macroeconomic environment, including the level of economic activity, inflation, exchange rates, and interest rates. At another level are the wide range of government rules and regulations that affect the opportunity and how resources are marshaled to exploit it. Examples extend from tax policy to the rules about raising capital for a private or public company. And at yet another level are factors like technology that define the limits of what a business or its competitors can accomplish.

Context often has a tremendous impact on every aspect of the entrepreneurial process, from identification of opportunity to harvest. In some cases, changes in some contextual factor create opportunity. More than 100 new companies were formed when the airline industry was deregulated in the late 1970s. The context for financing was also favorable, enabling new entrants like People Express to go to the public market for capital even before starting operations.

Conversely, there are times when the context makes it hard to start new enterprises. The recession of the early 1990s combined with a difficult financing environment for new companies: venture capital disbursements were low, as was the amount of capital raised in the public markets. (Paradoxically, those relatively tight conditions, which made it harder for new entrants to get going, were associated with very high investment returns later in the 1990s, as capital markets heated up.)

Sometimes, a shift in context turns an unattractive business into an attractive one, and vice versa. Consider the case of a packaging company some years ago that was performing so poorly it was about to be put on the block. Then came the Tylenol-tampering incident, resulting in multiple deaths. The packaging company happened to have an efficient mechanism for installing tamper-proof seals, and in a matter of weeks its financial performance could have been called spectacular. Conversely, U.S. tax reforms enacted in 1986 created havoc for companies in the real estate business, eliminating almost every positive incentive to invest. Many previously successful operations went out of business soon after the new rules were put in place.

Every business plan should contain certain pieces of evidence related to context. First, the entrepreneurs should show a heightened awareness of the new venture's context and how it helps or hinders their specific proposal. Second, and more important, they should demonstrate that they know the venture's context will inevitably change and describe how those changes might affect the business. Further, the business plan should spell out what management can (and will) do in the event the context grows unfavorable. Finally, the business plan should explain the ways (if any) in which management can affect context in a positive way. For example, management might be able to have an impact on regulations or on industry standards through lobbying efforts.

## Risk and Reward

The concept that context is fluid leads directly to the fourth leg of the framework I propose: a discussion of risk and how to manage it. I've come to think of a good business plan as a snapshot of an event in the future. That's quite a feat to begin with—taking a picture of the unknown. But the best business plans go beyond that; they are like movies of the future. They show the people, the opportunity, and the context from multiple angles. They offer a plausible, coherent story of what lies ahead. They unfold possibilities of action and reaction.

Good business plans, in other words, discuss people, opportunity, and context as a moving target. All three factors (and the relationship among them) are likely to change over time as a company evolves from start-up to ongoing enterprise. Therefore, any business plan worth the time it takes to write or read needs to focus attention on the dynamic aspects of the entrepreneurial process.

Of course, the future is hard to predict. Still, it is possible to give potential investors a sense of the kind and class of risk and reward they are assuming with a new venture. All it takes is a pencil and two simple drawings. (See "Visualizing Risk and Reward" on page 54.) But even with these drawings, risk is, well, risky. In reality, there are no immutable distributions of outcomes. It is ultimately the responsibility of management to change the distribution, to increase the likelihood and consequences of success, and to decrease the likelihood and implications of problems.

> *One of the greatest myths about entrepreneurs is that they are risk seekers. All sane people want to avoid risk.*

One of the great myths about entrepreneurs is that they are risk seekers. All sane people want to avoid risk. As Harvard Business School professor (and venture capitalist) Howard Stevenson says, true entrepreneurs want to capture all the reward and give all the risk to others. The best business is a post office box to which people send cashier's checks. Yet risk is unavoidable. So what does that mean for a business plan?

> *The best business is a post office box to which people send cashier's checks.*

It means that the plan must unflinchingly confront the risks ahead—in terms of people, opportunity, and context. What happens if one of the new venture's leaders leaves? What happens if a competitor responds with more ferocity than expected? What happens if there is a revolution in Namibia, the source of a key raw material? What will management actually *do?*

Those are hard questions for an entrepreneur to pose, especially when seeking capital. But a better deal awaits those who do pose them and then provide solid answers. A new venture, for example, might be highly leveraged and therefore very sensitive to interest rates. Its business plan would benefit enormously by stating that management intends to hedge its exposure through the financial-futures market by purchasing a contract that does well when interest rates go up. That is the equivalent of offering investors insurance. (It also makes sense for the business itself.)

Finally, one important area in the realm of risk/reward management relates to harvesting. Venture capitalists often ask if a company is "IPOable," by which they mean, Can the company be taken public at some point in the future? Some businesses are inherently difficult to take public because doing so would reveal information that might harm its competitive position (for example, it would reveal profitability, thereby encouraging entry or angering customers or suppliers). Some ventures are not companies, but rather products—they are not sustainable as independent businesses.

Therefore, the business plan should talk candidly about the end of the process. How will the investor eventually get money out of the business, assuming it is successful, even if only marginally so? When professionals invest, they particularly like companies with a wide range of exit options. They like companies that work hard to preserve and enhance those options along the way, companies that don't, for example, unthinkingly form alliances with big corporations that could someday actually *buy* them. Investors feel a lot better about risk if the venture's endgame is discussed up front. There is an old saying, "If you don't know where you are going, any road will get you there." In crafting sensible entrepreneurial strategies, just the opposite is true: you had better know where you might end up and have a map for getting there. A business plan should be the place where that map is drawn, for, as every traveler knows, a journey is a lot less risky when you have directions.

## The Deal and Beyond

Once a business plan is written, of course, the goal is to land a deal. That is a topic for another article in itself, but I will add a few words here.

When I talk to young (and old) entrepreneurs looking to finance their ventures, they obsess about the valuation and terms of the deal they will receive. Their explicit goal seems to be to minimize the dilution they will suffer in raising capital. Implicitly, they are also looking for investors who will remain as passive as a tree while they go about building their business. On the food chain of investors, it seems, doctors and dentists are best and venture capitalists are worst because of the degree to which the latter group demands control and a large share of the returns.

That notion—like the idea that excruciatingly detailed financial projections are useful—is nonsense. From whom you raise capital is often more important than the terms. New ventures are inherently risky, as I've noted; what can go wrong will. When that happens, unsophisticated investors panic, get angry, and often refuse to advance the company more money. Sophisticated investors, by contrast, roll up their sleeves and help the company solve its problems. Often, they've had lots of experience saving sinking ships. They are typically process literate. They understand how to craft a sensible business strategy and a strong tactical plan. They know how to recruit, compensate, and motivate team members. They are also familiar with the Byzantine ins and outs of going public—an event most entrepreneurs face but once in a lifetime. This kind of know-how is worth the money needed to buy it.

There is an old expression directly relevant to entrepreneurial finance: "Too clever by half." Often, deal makers get very creative, crafting all sorts of payoff and option schemes. That usually backfires. My experience has proven again and again that sensible deals have the following six characteristics:

- They are simple.
- They are fair.
- They emphasize trust rather than legal ties.
- They do not blow apart if actual differs slightly from plan.
- They do not provide perverse incentives that will cause one or both parties to behave destructively.
- They are written on a pile of papers no greater than one-quarter-inch thick.

But even these six simple rules miss an important point. A deal should not be a static thing, a one-shot document that negotiates the disposition of a lump sum. Instead, it is incumbent upon entrepreneurs, before they go searching for funding, to think about capital acquisition as a dynamic process—to figure out how much money they will need and when they will need it.

How is that accomplished? The trick is for the entrepreneurial team to treat the new venture as a series of experiments. Before launching the whole show, launch a little piece of it. Convene a focus group to test the product, build a prototype and watch it perform, conduct a regional or local rollout of a service. Such an exercise reveals the true economics of the business and can help enormously in determining how much money the new venture actually requires and in what stages. Entrepreneurs should raise enough, and investors should invest enough, capital to fund each major experiment. Experiments, of course, can feel expensive and risky. But I've seen them prevent disasters and help create successes. I consider it a prerequisite of putting together a winning deal.

## Beware the Albatross

Among the many sins committed by business plan writers is arrogance. In today's economy, few ideas are truly proprietary. Moreover, there has never been a time in recorded history when the supply of capital did not outrace the supply of opportunity. The true half-life of opportunity is decreasing with the passage of time.

A business plan must not be an albatross that hangs around the neck of the entrepreneurial team, dragging it into oblivion. Instead, a business plan must be a call for action, one that recognizes management's responsibility to fix what is broken proactively and in real time. Risk is inevitable, avoiding risk impossible. Risk management is the key, always tilting the venture in favor of reward and away from risk.

A plan must demonstrate mastery of the entire entrepreneurial process, from identification of opportunity to harvest. It is not a way to separate unsuspecting investors from their money by hiding the fatal flaw. For in the final analysis, the only one being fooled is the entrepreneur.

We live today in the golden age of entrepreneurship. Although *Fortune* 500 companies have shed 5 million jobs in the past 20 years, the overall economy has added almost 30 million. Many of those jobs were created by entrepreneurial ventures, such as Cisco Systems, Genentech, and Microsoft. Each of those companies started with a business plan. Is that why they succeeded? There is no knowing for sure. But there is little doubt that crafting a business plan so that it thoroughly and candidly addresses the ingredients of success—people, opportunity, context, and the risk/reward picture—is vitally important. In the absence of a crystal ball, in fact, a business plan built of the *right* information and analysis can only be called indispensable.

---

## Business Plans: For Entrepreneurs Only?

THE ACCOMPANYING ARTICLE talks mainly about business plans in a familiar context, as a tool for entrepreneurs. But quite often, start-ups are launched within established companies. Do those new ventures require business plans? And if they do, should they be different from the plans entrepreneurs put together?

The answer to the first question is an emphatic yes; the answer to the second, an equally emphatic no. All new ventures—whether they are funded by venture capitalists or, as is the case with intrapreneurial businesses, by shareholders—need to pass the same acid tests. After all, the marketplace does not differentiate between products or services based on who is pouring money into them behind the scenes.

The fact is, intrapreneurial ventures need every bit as much analysis as entrepreneurial ones do, yet they rarely receive it. Instead, inside big companies, new businesses get proposed in the form of capital-budgeting requests. These faceless documents are subject to detailed financial scrutiny and a consensus-building process, as the project wends its way through the chain of command, what I call the "neutron bomb" model of project governance. However, in the history of such proposals, a plan never has been submitted that did not promise returns in excess of corporate hurdle rates. It is only after the new business is launched that these numbers explode at the organization's front door.

That problem could be avoided in large part if intrapreneurial ventures followed the guidelines set out in the accompanying article. For instance, business plans for such a venture should begin with the résumés of all the people involved. What has the team done in the past that would suggest it would be successful in the future, and so on? In addition, the new venture's product or service should be fully analyzed in terms of its opportunity and context. Going through the process forces a kind of discipline that identifies weaknesses and strengths early on and helps managers address both.

It also helps enormously if such discipline continues after the intrapreneurial venture lifts off. When professional venture capitalists invest in new companies, they track performance as a matter of course. But in large companies, scrutiny of a new venture is often inconsistent. That shouldn't or needn't be the case. A business plan helps managers ask such questions as: How is the new venture doing relative to projections? What decisions has the team made in response to new information? Have changes in the context made additional funding necessary? How could the team have predicted those changes? Such questions not only keep a new venture running smoothly but also help an organization learn from its mistakes and triumphs.

Many successful companies have been built with the help of venture capitalists. Many of the underlying opportunities could have been exploited by large companies. Why weren't they? Perhaps useful lessons can be learned by studying the world of independent ventures, one lesson being: Write a great business plan.

## A Glossary of Business Plan Terms

| What They Say . . . | and What They Really Mean |
| --- | --- |
| We conservatively project . . . | We read a book that said we had to be a $50 million company in five years, and we reverse-engineered the numbers. |
| We took our best guess and divided by 2. | We accidentally divided by 0.5. |
| We project a 10% margin. | We did not modify any of the assumptions in the business plan template that we downloaded from the Internet. |

| What They Say . . . | and What They Really Mean |
|---|---|
| The project is 98% complete. | To complete the remaining 2% will take as long as it took to create the initial 98% but will cost twice as much. |
| Our business model is proven . . . | if you take the evidence from the past week for the best of our 50 locations and extrapolate it for all the others. |
| We have a six-month lead. | We tried not to find out how many other people have a six-month lead. |
| We only need a 10% market-share. | So do the other 50 entrants getting funded. |
| Customers are clamoring for our product. | We have not yet asked them to pay for it. Also, all of our current customers are relatives. |
| We are the low-cost producer. | We have not produced anything yet, but we are confident that we will be able to. |
| We have no competition. | Only IBM, Microsoft, Netscape, and Sun have announced plans to enter the business. |
| Our management team has a great deal of experience . . . | consuming the product or service. |
| A select group of investors is considering the plan. | We mailed a copy of the plan to everyone in Pratt's Guide. |
| We seek a value-added investor. | We are looking for a passive, dumb-as-rocks investor. |
| If you invest on our terms, you will earn a 68% internal rate of return. | If everything that could ever conceivably go right does go right, you might get your money back. |

# Who Are These People, Anyway?

### Fourteen "Personal" Questions Every Business Plan Should Answer

- Where are the founders from?
- Where have they been educated?
- Where have they worked—and for whom?
- What have they accomplished—professionally and personally—in the past?
- What is their reputation within the business community?
- What experience do they have that is directly relevant to the opportunity they are pursuing?
- What skills, abilities, and knowledge do they have?
- How realistic are they about the venture's chances for success and the tribulations it will face?
- Who else needs to be on the team?
- Are they prepared to recruit high-quality people?
- How will they respond to adversity?
- Do they have the mettle to make the inevitable hard choices that have to be made?
- How committed are they to this venture?
- What are their motivations?

---

# The Opportunity of a Lifetime—or Is It?

### Nine Questions About the Business Every Business Plan Should Answer

- Who is the new venture's customer?

- How does the customer make decisions about buying this product or service?

- To what degree is the product or service a compelling purchase for the customer?

- How will the product or service be priced?

- How will the venture reach all the identified customer segments?

- How much does it cost (in time and resources) to acquire a customer?

- How much does it cost to produce and deliver the product or service?

- How much does it cost to support a customer?

- How easy is it to retain a customer?

---

# Visualizing Risk and Reward

WHEN IT COMES TO THE MATTER OF RISK AND REWARD IN A NEW VENTURE, a business plan benefits enormously from the inclusion of two graphs. Perhaps *graphs* is the wrong word; these are really just schematic pictures that illustrate the most likely relationship between risk and reward, that is, the relationship between the opportunity and its economics. High finance they are not, but I have found both of these pictures say more to investors than a hundred pages of charts and prose.

The first picture depicts the amount of money needed to launch the new venture, time to positive cash flow, and the expected magnitude of the payoff.

This image helps the investor understand the depth and duration of negative cash flow, as well as the relationship between the investment and the possible return. The ideal, needless to say, is to have cash flow early and often. But most investors are intrigued by the picture even when the cash outflow is high and long—as long as the cash inflow is more so.

Of course, since the world of new ventures is populated by wild-eyed optimists, you might expect the picture

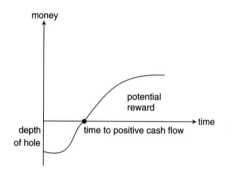

to display a shallower hole and a steeper reward slope than it should. It usually does. But to be honest, even that kind of picture belongs in the business plan because it is a fair warning to investors that the new venture's team is completely out of touch with reality and should be avoided at all costs.

The second picture complements the first. It shows investors the range of possible returns and the likelihood of achieving them. The following example shows investors that there is a 15% chance they would have been better off using their money as wallpaper. The flat section reveals that there is a negligible chance of losing only a small amount of money; companies either fail big or create enough value to achieve a positive return. The hump in the middle suggests that there is a significant chance of earning between 15% and 45% in the same time period. And finally, there is a small chance that the initial outlay of cash will spawn a 200% internal rate of return, which might have occurred if you had happened to invest in Microsoft when it was a private company.

Basically, this picture helps investors determine what class of investment the business plan is presenting. Is the new venture drilling for North Sea oil—highly risky with

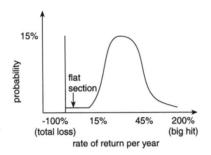

potentially big payoffs—or is it digging development wells in Texas, which happens to be less of a geological gamble and probably less lucrative, too? This image answers that kind of question. It's then up to the investors to decide how much risk they want to live with against what kind of odds.

Again, the people who write business plans might be inclined to skew the picture to make it look as if the probability of a significant return is downright huge and the possibility of loss is negligible. And, again, I would say therein lies the picture's beauty. What it claims, checked against the investor's sense of reality and experience, should serve as a simple pictorial caveat emptor.

**Originally published in July–August 1997**
**Reprint 97409**

# How Entrepreneurs Craft Strategies That Work

AMAR BHIDE

## Executive Summary

HOWEVER POPULAR COMPREHENSIVE RESEARCH AND PLANNING may be in some business arenas, they don't suit the fast-moving environment of start-ups. Entrepreneurs must move quickly on their ideas or opportunities may no longer exist. Theirs is a world of ingenuity, spontaneity, and hustle. Profitable survival requires an edge derived from some combination of a creative idea and a superior capacity for execution. Instead of in-depth analysis, therefore, successful entrepreneurs adopt practical approaches that are quick, inexpensive, and timely.

Research on more than 200 thriving ventures reveal four helpful guidelines for aspiring founders. First, effective entrepreneurs screen out unpromising ideas as early as possible, and they accomplish this through judgment and reflection, not gathering lots of data. Next, they assess realistically their financial situation, personal preferences, and goals for the venture. In this way, they gauge the attractiveness of an idea and choose just the right new enterprise for them. Surviving the inevitable disappointments on the rough road to success requires a passion for the business.

To conserve time and money, successful new founders also minimize the resources they devote to researching ideas. The appropriate analytical priorities will vary for each venture. And, unlike managers in big corporations, entrepreneurs don't need all the answers to act. In fact, analyzing and acting are tough to separate in entrepreneurial environments. Smart founders dive in and improvise, and as soon as problems arise, they begin looking for solutions. They plug holes quickly and change strategies as events unfold.

---

However popular it may be in the corporate world, a comprehensive analytical approach to planning doesn't suit most start-ups. Entrepreneurs typically lack the time and money to interview a representative cross section of potential customers, let alone analyze substitutes, reconstruct competitors' cost structures, or project alternative technology scenarios. In fact, too much analysis can be harmful; by the time an opportunity is investigated fully, it may no longer exist. A city map and restaurant guide on a CD may be a winner in January but worthless if delayed until December.

*By the time an opportunity is investigated fully, it may no longer exist.*

Interviews with the founders of 100 companies on the 1989 *Inc.* "500" list of the fastest growing private companies in the United States and recent research on more than 100 other thriving ventures by my MBA students suggest that many successful entrepreneurs spend little time researching and analyzing. (See "Does Planning Pay?" on page 84.) And those who do often have to scrap their strategies and start over. Furthermore, a 1990 National Federation of Independent Business study of 2,994 start-ups showed that founders who spent a long time in study, reflection, and planning were no more likely to survive their first three years than people who seized opportunities without planning. In fact, many corporations that revere comprehensive analysis develop a refined incapacity for seizing opportunities. Analysis can delay entry until it's too late or kill ideas by identifying numerous problems.

Yet all ventures merit some analysis and planning. Appearances to the contrary, successful entrepreneurs don't take risks blindly. Rather, they use a quick, cheap approach that represents a middle ground between planning paralysis and no planning at all. They don't expect perfection—even the most astute entrepreneurs have their share of false starts. Compared to typical corporate practice, however, the entrepreneurial approach is more economical and timely.

What are the critical elements of winning entrepreneurial approaches? Our evidence suggests three general guidelines for aspiring founders:

1. Screen opportunities quickly to weed out unpromising ventures.

2. Analyze ideas parsimoniously. Focus on a few important issues.

3. Integrate action and analysis. Don't wait for all the answers, and be ready to change course.

## Screening Out Losers

Individuals who seek entrepreneurial opportunities usually generate lots of ideas. Quickly discarding those that have low potential frees aspirants to concentrate on the few ideas that merit refinement and study.

Screening out unpromising ventures requires judgment and reflection, not new data. The entrepreneur should already be familiar with the facts needed to determine whether an idea has prima facie merit. Our evidence suggests that new ventures are usually started to solve problems the founders have grappled with personally as customers or employees. (See the diagram "Where

### Where Do Entrepreneurs Get Their Ideas?

Discovered through systematic research for opportunities

Swept into the PC revolution

Discovered serendipitously:

Built temporary or casual job into a business (7%)

Wanted as an individual consumer (6%)

Happened to read about the industry (4%)

Developed family member's idea (2%)

Thought up during honeymoon in Italy (1%)

Replicated or modified an idea encountered through previous employment

4%
5%
20%
71%

Source: 100 founders of the 1989 Inc. "500" fastest growing private companies.

Do Entrepreneurs Get Their Ideas?") Companies like Federal Express, which grew out of a paper its founder wrote in college, are rare.

Profitable survival requires an edge derived from some combination of a creative idea and a superior capacity for execution. (See the diagram "Tipping the Competitive Balance.") The entrepreneur's creativity may involve an innovative product or a process that changes the existing order. Or the entrepreneur may have a unique insight about the course or consequence of an external change: the California gold rush, for

*There is no ideal profile. Entrepreneurs can be gregarious or taciturn, analytical or intuitive, cautious or daring.*

example, made paupers of the thousands caught in the frenzy, but Levi Strauss started a company—and a legend—by recognizing the opportunity to supply rugged canvas and later denim trousers to prospectors.

But entrepreneurs cannot rely on just inventing new products or anticipating a trend. They must also execute well, especially if their concepts can be copied easily. For example, if an innovation cannot be patented or kept

---

## Tipping the Competitive Balance

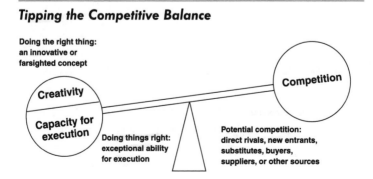

Doing the right thing: an innovative or farsighted concept

Creativity

Capacity for execution

Doing things right: exceptional ability for execution

Competition

Potential competition: direct rivals, new entrants, substitutes, buyers, suppliers, or other sources

secret, entrepreneurs must acquire and manage the resources needed to build a brand name or other barriers that will deter imitators. Superior execution can also compensate for a me-too concept in emerging or rapidly growing industries where doing it quickly and doing it right are more important than brilliant strategy.

Ventures that obviously lack a creative concept or any special capacity to execute—the ex-consultant's scheme to exploit grandmother's cookie recipe, for instance—can be discarded without much thought. In other cases, entrepreneurs must reflect on the adequacy of their ideas and their capacities to execute them.

Successful start-ups don't need an edge on every front. The creativity of successful entrepreneurs varies considerably. Some implement a radical idea, some modify, and some show no originality. Capacity for execution also varies among entrepreneurs. Selling an industrial niche product doesn't call for the charisma that's required to pitch trinkets through infomercials. Our evidence suggests that there is no ideal entrepreneurial profile either: successful founders can be gregarious or taciturn, analytical or intuitive, good or terrible with details, risk averse or thrill seeking. They can be delegators or control freaks, pillars of the community or outsiders. In assessing the viability of a potential venture, therefore, each aspiring entrepreneur should consider three interacting factors:

**1. Objectives of the Venture.** Is the entrepreneur's goal to build a large, enduring enterprise, carve out a niche, or merely turn a quick profit? Ambitious goals require great creativity. Building a large enterprise quickly, either by seizing a significant share of an existing market or by creating a large new market, usually calls for a revolutionary idea. Launching Home Depot, for example, called for a new retailing concept of immense proportions; opening a traditional hardware store does not. Revolutionary enterprises usually require new processes or manufacturing techniques; competitive markets rarely fail to provide valuable products or services unless providing them involves serious technological problems.

Requirements for execution are also stiff. Big ideas often necessitate big money and strong organizations. Successful entrepreneurs, therefore, require an evangelical ability to attract, retain, and balance the interests of investors, customers, employees, and suppliers for a seemingly outlandish vision, as well as the organizational and leadership skills to build a large, complex company quickly. In addition, the entrepreneur may require considerable technical know-how in deal making, strategic planning, managing overhead, and other business skills. The revolutionary entrepreneur, in other words, would appear to require almost superhuman qualities: ordinary mortals need not apply.

Consider Federal Express founder Fred Smith. His creativity lay in recognizing that customers would pay a significant premium for reliable overnight delivery and in figuring out a way to provide the service for them. Smith ruled out using existing commercial flights, whose schedules were designed to serve passenger traffic. Instead, he had the audacious idea of acquiring a dedicated fleet of jets and shipping all packages through a central hub that was located in Memphis.

As with most big ideas, the concept was difficult to execute. Smith, 28 years old at the time, had to raise $91 million in venture funding. The jets, the hub, operations in 25 states, and several hundred trained employees had to be in place before the company could open for business. And Smith needed great fortitude and skill to prevent the fledgling enterprise from going under: Federal Express lost over $40 million in its first three years. Some investors tried to remove Smith, and creditors tried to seize assets. Yet Smith somehow preserved morale and mollified investors and lenders while the company expanded its operations and launched national advertising and direct-mail campaigns to build market share.

In contrast, ventures that seek to capture a market niche, not transform or create an industry, don't need extraordinary ideas. Some ingenuity is necessary to design a product that will draw customers away from mainstream offerings and overcome the cost penalty of serving a small market. But features that are too novel can be a hindrance; a niche market will rarely justify the investment required to educate customers and distributors about the benefits of a radically new product.

*Entrepreneurs at International Record Syndicate built customer awareness through guerrilla marketing on MTV Music Television.*

Similarly, a niche venture cannot support too much production or distribution innovation; unlike Federal Express, the Cape Cod Potato Chip Company, for example, must work within the limits of its distributors and truckers.

And since niche markets cannot support much investment or overhead, entrepreneurs do not need the revolutionary's ability to raise capital and build large organizations. Rather, the entrepreneur must be able to secure others' resources on favorable terms and make do with less, building brand awareness through guerrilla marketing and word of mouth instead of national advertising, for example.

Jay Boberg and Miles Copeland, who launched International Record Syndicate (IRS) in 1979, used a niche strategy, my students Elisabeth Bentel and Victoria Hackett found, to create one of the most successful new music labels in North America. Lacking the funds or a great innovation to compete against the major labels, Boberg and Copeland promoted "alternative" music—undiscovered British groups like the Buzzcocks and Skafish—which the major labels were ignoring because their potential sales were too small. And IRS used low-cost, alternative marketing methods to promote their alternative music. At the time, the major record labels had not yet realized that music videos on television could be used effectively to promote their products. Boberg, however, jumped at the opportunity to produce a rock show, "The Cutting Edge," for MTV. The show proved to be a hit with fans and an effective promotional tool for IRS. Before "The Cutting Edge," Boberg had to plead with radio stations to play his songs. Afterward, the MTV audience demanded that disc jockeys play the songs they had heard on the show.

**2. Leverage Provided by External Change.** Exploiting opportunities in a new or changing industry is generally easier than making waves in a mature industry. Enormous creativity, experience, and contacts are needed to take business away from competitors in a mature industry, where market forces have long shaken out weak technologies, strategies, and organizations.

But new markets are different. There start-ups often face rough-around-the-edges rivals, customers who tolerate inexperienced vendors and imperfect products, and opportunities to profit from shortages. Small insights and marginal innovations, a little skill or expertise (in the land of the blind, the one-eyed person is king), and the willingness to act quickly can go a long way. In fact, with great external uncertainty, customers and investors may be hesitant to back a radical product and technology until the environment settles down. Strategic choices in a new industry are often very limited; entrepreneurs have to adhere to the emerging standards for product features, components, or distribution channels.

*External changes can provide great leverage for creative and nimble entrepreneurs.*

The leverage provided by external change is illustrated by the success of numerous start-ups in hardware, software, training, retailing, and systems integration that emerged from the personal computer revolution of the 1980s. Installing or fixing a computer system is probably easier than repairing a car; but because people with the initiative or foresight to acquire the skill were scarce, entrepreneurs like Bohdan's Peter Zacharkiw built successful dealerships by providing what customers saw as exceptional service (see "Does Planning Pay?" on page 84). As one Midwestern dealer told me, "We have a joke slogan around here: We aren't as incompetent as our competitors!"

*Microsoft's Bill Gates built a multibillion-dollar business without a breakthrough product.*

Bill Gates turned Microsoft into a multibillion-dollar company without a breakthrough product by showing up in the industry early and capitalizing on the opportunities that came his way. Gates, then 19, and his partner

Paul Allen, 21, launched Microsoft in 1975 to sell software they had created. By 1979, Microsoft had grown to 25 employees and $2.5 million in sales. Then in November 1980, IBM chose Microsoft to provide an operating system for its personal computer. Microsoft thereupon bought an operating system from Seattle Computer Products, which it modified into the now ubiquitous MS-DOS. The IBM name and the huge success of the 1–2–3 spreadsheet, which only ran on DOS computers, soon helped make Microsoft the dominant supplier of operating systems.

Microsoft won the operating system battle without clockwork execution and amidst considerable organizational turmoil. According to author Scott Lewis, during the early 1980s, "The firm was doubling in size every year and had not yet adapted to being a large company. Gates, whose volatile temperament was well known in the computer industry, had exacerbated Microsoft's chaos by abruptly changing product specifications and moving developers around."[1]

External changes, such as collapses in the price of real estate or energy, also create opportunities for entrepreneurs who speculate in out-of-favor assets. Sam Zell, the self-described "grave dancer," and his now deceased partner, Robert Lurie, built a multibillion-dolar real estate and industrial empire through such opportunities. Their first big success followed the collapse of the real estate investment trusts in the early 1970s. Later they picked up millions of square feet of office space and shopping centers and tens of thousands of apartments and trailer-park spaces for mobile homes. During the early 1980s, the partners sold a number of buildings in the booming Southwest and invested in Rust Belt cities like Buffalo and Chicago.

His approach, Zell concedes, doesn't call for the sort of creativity that's involved in building a business.[2] Contrarian speculators don't innovate much; the entrepreneur merely anticipates that the confusion or panic that has depressed prices will pass. Nor does successful execution require much managerial capacity. Organizational development, engineering, or marketing abilities add little value when an entrepreneur buys assets at a low price, expecting to sell them at a high price. Rather, good execution requires the ability to move quickly, negotiate astutely, and raise funds under favorable terms.

**3. Basis of Competition: Proprietary Assets Versus Hustle.** In some industries, such as pharmaceuticals, luxury hotels, and consumer goods, a company's profitability depends significantly on the assets it owns or controls—patents, location, or brands, for example. Good management practices like listening to customers, maintaining quality, and paying attention to costs, which can improve the profits of a going business, cannot propel a start-up over such structural barriers. Here a creative new technology, product, or strategy is a must.

Companies in fragmented service industries, such as investment management, investment banking, head hunting, or consulting cannot establish proprietary advantages easily but can nonetheless enjoy high profits by providing exceptional service tailored to client demands. Start-ups in those fields rely mainly on their hustle.[3] Successful entrepreneurs depend on personal selling skills, contacts, their reputa-

*McKinsey & Company grew out of a simple idea: high-quality advice for top managers.*

tions for expertise, and their ability to convince clients of the value of the services rendered. They also have the capacity for institution building—skills such as recruiting and motivating stellar professionals and articulating and reinforcing company values. Where there are few natural economies of scale, an entrepreneur cannot create a going concern out of a one-man-band or ad hoc ensemble without a lot of expertise in organizational development.

Marvin Bower, who cofounded McKinsey & Company in 1939, created a premier management consulting firm through the relentless execution of a simple idea: providing high-quality business advice to the top managers of large companies. Bower was very skilled in developing and serving his clients and was dogged in building organizational capabilities. He preached constantly the virtues of putting clients' interests first. Under his leadership, McKinsey started recruiting from top business schools, adopted an up-or-out policy to eliminate employees who didn't make the mark, declined studies that didn't fit the firm's mission of serving top management, and opened international offices to better serve chosen clientele. Bower didn't dictate policy, however, and had the patience to work on bringing partners around to his point of view. Also, he was willing to sell his stock at book value so that the equity of the firm was shared widely.[4]

## Gauging Attractiveness

Entrepreneurs should also screen potential ventures for their attractiveness—their risks and rewards—compared to other opportunities. Several factors should be considered. Capital requirements, for example, matter to the entrepreneur who lacks easy access to financial markets. An unexpected need for cash because, say, one large customer is unable to make a timely payment may shut down a venture or force a fire sale of the founder's equity. Therefore, entrepreneurs should favor ventures that aren't capital intensive and have the profit margins to sustain rapid growth with internally generated funds. In a similar fashion, entrepreneurs should look for a high margin for error, ventures with simple operations and low fixed costs that are less likely to face a cash crunch because of factors such as technical delays, cost overruns, and slow buildup of sales.

*An attractive venture should provide a substantial enough reward to compensate the entrepreneur's exclusive commitment to it.*

Other criteria reflect the typical entrepreneur's inability to undertake multiple projects: an attractive venture should provide a substantial enough reward to compensate the entrepreneur's exclusive commitment to it. Shut-down costs should be low: the payback should be quick, or failure soon recognized so that the venture can be terminated without a significant loss of time, money, or reputation. And the entrepreneur should have the option to cash in, for example, by selling all or part of the equity. An entrepreneur locked into an illiquid business cannot easily pursue other opportunities and risks fatigue and burnout.

*Surviving the inevitable disappointments on the rough road to success requires passion for the chosen business.*

These criteria cannot be applied mechanically like, say, a textbook rule of backing all projects with positive net present value (NPV). Ventures that shine by one measure are often questionable by another. For example, a successful biotech venture whose patents provide sustainable advantages can be taken public more easily than an advertising agency. But biotech entrepreneurs need to raise significant capital and may be locked into a venture whose success can't be ascertained for many years.

Ventures must also fit what the individual entrepreneur values and wants to do. Surviving the inevitable disappointments and near disasters one encounters on the rough road to success requires a passion for the chosen business. Entrepreneurs should evaluate a potential new venture against what they're looking for and the sacrifices they're willing to make. Do they want to make a fortune, or will a small profit be sufficient? Do they seek public recognition? Is the stimulation of working with exciting technologies, customers, or colleagues important to them? Are they prepared to devote their lives to a business, or do they want to cash out quickly? Can they tolerate working in an industry that has questionable ethical standards? Or an industry where there is high uncertainty? What financial and career risks are they prepared to take and for how long?

These deeply personal preferences determine the types of ventures that will enthuse and fortify an entrepreneur. For example, ambitious undertakings like Federal Express fit people who are ready to win or lose on a grand scale. Success can create dynastic fortunes and turn the entrepreneur into a near-cult figure. But the risks also are substantial. Visionary schemes may fail for any number of reasons: the product is flawed, cannot be made or distributed cost-effectively, serves no compelling need, or requires customers to incur unacceptable switching costs. Worse, the failure may not be apparent for several years, locking the entrepreneur into an extended period of frustrating endeavor. Even businesses that succeed may not be financially rewarding for their founders, especially if they encounter delays en route. Investors may dump the visionary founders or demand a high share of the equity for additional financing. The entrepreneur must therefore anticipate recurring disappointments and a high probability that years of toil may come to naught. Unless entrepreneurs have a burning desire to change the world, they should not undertake revolutionary ventures.

Surprisingly, small endeavors often hold more financial promise than large ones. Often the founders can keep a larger share of the profits because they don't dilute their equity interest through multiple rounds of financings. But entrepreneurs must be willing to prosper in a backwater; dominating a neglected market segment is sometimes more profitable than intellectually stimulating or glamorous. Niche enterprises can also enter the "land of the living dead" because their market is too small for the business to thrive but the entrepreneur has invested too much effort to be willing to quit.

Speculators like Zell, who don't build a company or introduce an innovation to the world, can take pleasure from showing up the crowd. Their financial risks and returns depend on the terms of the deal, the capital at risk, the conditions and amount of borrowing, and, of course, the price of the asset acquired. Risks are generally not staged; the entrepreneur is fully exposed when the asset is acquired. Liquidity or exit options often turn on the success of the speculation: if, as hoped, prices rise, the speculator can expect many buyers for the asset owned, but if prices decline or stay depressed, market liquidity for the asset will be generally poor. All things considered, such ventures appeal most to entrepreneurs who enjoy making deals and rolling the dice.

A new company that is based on hustle in, say, consulting or advertising can provide the satisfaction of working with talented colleagues in a dynamic and competitive market. Capital requirements are low, and investments can be staged as the business grows. Entrepreneurs can therefore avoid significant personal risk and meddling by outside investors. But although such businesses can provide attractive current income, great wealth in those situations is elusive: hustle businesses, which lack a sustainable franchise, cannot be easily sold or taken public at a high multiple of earnings. The entrepreneur must therefore savor the venture enough to make a long-term career of it rather than enjoy the fruits of a quick harvest.

## Parsimonious Planning and Analysis

To conserve time and money, successful entrepreneurs minimize the resources they devote to researching their ideas. Unlike the corporate world, where foil mastery and completed staff work can make a career, the entrepreneur only does as much planning and analysis as seems useful and makes subjective judgment calls when necessary.

As Harvard's Michael Porter has pointed out, a start-up faces competition not only from rivals offering the same goods but also potentially from substitutes, suppliers, buyers, and other new entrants. A start-up even competes with companies outside its industry for employees and capital. A complete analysis, therefore, would cover many industry participants and probe internal core competencies and weaknesses. But the

astute entrepreneur isn't interested in completeness. He
or she understands that returns from additional analysis
diminish rapidly and avoids using spreadsheet software
to churn out detailed but not particularly insightful
analyses of a project's break-even point, capital requirements, payback period, or NPV.

In setting their analytical priorities, entrepreneurs
must recognize that some critical uncertainties cannot
be resolved through more research. For example, focus
groups and surveys often
have little value in pre-
dicting demand for
products that are truly
novel. At first, con-
sumers had dismissed
the need for copiers, for
instance, and told researchers they were satisfied with
using carbon paper. With issues like this, entrepreneurs
have to resist the temptation of endless investigation
and trust their judgment.

*Standard checklists or one-size-fits-all approaches don't work. The appropriate analytical priorities vary for each venture.*

The parsimonious analyst should also avoid research
that he or she can't act on. For example, understanding
broad market trends and the strategies of the industry
leaders is unlikely to affect what a start-up in a hustle
business like advertising does and therefore isn't worth
bothering with. Entrepreneurs should concentrate
instead on issues that they can reasonably expect to
resolve through analysis and that determine whether
and how they will proceed. Resolving a few big questions—understanding what things *must* go right and
anticipating the venture-destroying pitfalls, for
instance—is more important than investigating many
nice-to-know matters.

Standard checklists or one-size-fits-all approaches
don't work for entrepreneurs. The appropriate analytical

budget and the issues that are most worthy of research and analysis depend on the characteristics of each venture.

Ambitious endeavors like Federal Express, for example, require significant capital and must be better researched and documented than ventures that can be self-financed. Professional investors usually ask for a written business plan because it provides clues about the entrepreneur's seriousness of purpose, concern for investors, and competence. So entrepreneurs must write a detailed plan even if they are skeptical about its relationship to the subsequent outcomes.

Revenues are notoriously difficult to predict. At best, entrepreneurs may satisfy themselves that their novel product or service delivers considerably greater value than current offerings do; how quickly the product catches on is a blind guess. Leverage may be obtained, however, from analyzing how customers might buy and use the product or service. Understanding the purchase process can help identify the right decision makers for the new offering. With Federal Express, for instance, it was important to go beyond the mailroom managers who traditionally bought delivery services. Understanding how products are used can also help by revealing obstacles that must be overcome before consumers can benefit from a new offering.

*Start-ups with powerful competitors must wow their customers. A marginally tastier cereal won't knock Kellogg's Corn Flakes off supermarket shelves.*

Visionary entrepreneurs must guard against making competitors rich from their work. Many concepts are difficult to prove but, once proven, easy to imitate. Unless the pioneer is protected by sustainable barriers to entry, the benefits of a hard-fought revolution can become a public good rather than a boon to the innovator. Sun Microsystems and Apple, for example, won big from pathbreaking innovations that had been developed at Xerox's Palo Alto Research Center.

Entrepreneurs who hope to secure a niche face different problems: they often fail because the costs of serving a specialized segment exceed the benefits to customers. Entrepreneurs should therefore analyze carefully the incremental costs of serving a niche and take into account their lack of scale and the difficulty of marketing to a small, diffused segment. And especially if the cost disadvantage is significant, entrepreneurs should determine whether their offering provides a significant performance benefit. Whereas established companies can vie for share through line extensions or marginal tailoring of their products and services, the start-up must really wow its target customers. A marginally tastier cereal won't knock Kellogg's Corn Flakes off supermarket shelves.

Inadequate payoffs also pose a risk for ventures that address small markets. For example, a niche venture that can't support a direct sales force may not generate enough commissions to attract an independent broker or manufacturers' rep. Entrepreneurs will eventually lose interest too if the rewards aren't commensurate with their efforts. Therefore, the entrepreneur should make sure that everyone who contributes can expect a high, quick, or sustainable return even if the venture's total profits are small.

Entrepreneurs who seek to leverage factors like changing technologies, customer preferences, or regulations should avoid extensive analysis. Research conducted under conditions of such turbulence isn't reliable, and the importance of a quick response precludes spending the time to make sure every detail is covered.

The entrepreneur has to live with critical uncertainties, such as the relative competence of rivals or the preferences of strategic customers, which are not easy to analyze. Who could have forecast, for example, that Sun Microsystems's four 27–year-old founders, who had virtually no business or industry experience, would beat more than a dozen start-ups, including Apollo, a textbook venture launched by industry superstars? Or that IBM would turn to Microsoft for an operating system, gain dominance for its hardware, and go on to dethrone Digital Research's entrenched CP/M operating system? Entering a race requires faith in one's ability to finish ahead of whoever else might happen to play.

Analyzing whether or not the rewards for winning are commensurate with the risks, however, can be a more feasible and worthwhile exercise. In some technology races, success is predictably short-lived. In the disk-drive industry, for example, companies that succeed with one generation of products are often leap-frogged when the next generation arrives. In engineering workstations, however, Sun enjoyed long-term gains from its early success because it established a durable architectural standard. If success is unlikely to be sustained, entrepreneurs should have a plan for making a good return while it lasts.

Ventures in fast-changing markets are more likely to fold because they can't design, produce, or sell a timely, cost-effective product that works than because they pursued a poor strategy. Successful entrepreneurs, therefore, usually devote more attention to operational analysis and planning than strategic planning. Sun's business plan, one founder recalls, was mainly an operating plan, containing specific timetables for product development, opening sales and service offices, and hiring engineers.

For speculators like Zell who seek to purchase assets at depressed prices, two sets of analysis are crucial. One relates to the market dynamics for the asset being acquired or, more specifically, why the prices of the asset may be expected to rise. Entrepreneurs should try to determine whether prices are temporarily low (due to, say, an irrational panic or a temporary surge in supply), in secular decline because of permanent changes in supply or demand, or merely correcting after an irrational prior surge. Also important to analyze is the entrepreneur's ability to hold or carry the asset until it can be sold at a profit because it is difficult to predict when temporarily depressed prices will return to normal. Carrying capacity depends on the extent of borrowing used to purchase the asset, the conditions under which financing may be revoked, and the income produced by the asset. Rental properties or a producing well that provides ongoing income, for example, can be carried more easily than raw land or drilling rights. For certain kinds of assets, mines and urban rental properties, for example, the entrepreneur should also consider the risks of expropriation (through, for example, rent control) and windfall taxation.

In ventures based on hustle rather than proprietary advantages, a detailed analysis of competitors and industry structure is rarely of much value. The ability to seize short-lived opportunities and execute them brilliantly is of far more importance than a long-term competitive strategy. Analysis of specific clients and relationships dominates general market surveys. Partnership agreements, terms for offering equity to later

employees, performance measurement criteria, and
bonus plans are important determinants of company
success and are best thought through before launch
rather than hastily improvised later on. And although
projections of long-term cash flows are not meaningful,
back-of-the-envelope, short-term cash forecasts and
analyses of breakevens can keep the entrepreneur out of
trouble. Overall, though, the analytical preparation
required for such ventures is modest.

## Integrating Action and Analysis

Standard operating procedure in large corporations usually makes a clear distinction between analysis and execution. In contemplating a new venture, managers in
established companies face issues about its fit with
ongoing activities: Does the proposed venture leverage
corporate strengths? Will the resources and attention it
requires reduce the company's ability to build customer
loyalty and improve quality in core markets? These concerns dictate a deliberate, "trustee" approach: before
they can launch a venture, managers must investigate an
opportunity extensively, seek the counsel of people
higher up, submit a formal plan, respond to criticisms by
bosses and corporate staff, and secure a headcount and
capital allocation.[5]

Entrepreneurs who start with a clean slate, however,
don't have to know all the answers before they act. In
fact, they often can't easily separate action and analysis.
The attractiveness of a new restaurant, for example, may
depend on the terms of the lease; low rents can change
the venture from a mediocre proposition into a money
machine. But an entrepreneur's ability to negotiate a

good lease cannot be easily determined from a general prior analysis; he or she must enter into a serious negotiation with a specific landlord for a specific property.

Acting before an opportunity is fully analyzed has many benefits. Doing something concrete builds confidence in oneself and in others. Key employees and investors will often follow the individual who has committed to action, for instance, by quitting a job, incorporating, or signing a lease. By taking a personal risk, the entrepreneur convinces other people that the venture *will* proceed, and they may believe that if they don't sign up, they could be left behind.

Early action can generate more robust, better informed strategies too. Extensive surveys and focus-group research about a concept can produce misleading evidence: slippage can arise between research and reality because the potential customers interviewed are not representative of the market, their enthusiasm for the concept wanes when they see the actual product, or they lack the authority to sign purchase orders. More robust strategies may be developed by first building a working prototype and asking customers to use it before conducting extensive market research.

The ability of individual entrepreneurs to execute quickly will naturally vary. Trial and error is less feasible with large-scale, capital-intensive ventures like Orbital Sciences, which had to raise over $50 million to build rockets for NASA, than with a consulting firm start-up. Nevertheless, some characteristics are common to an approach that integrates action and analysis:

- **Handling Analytical Tasks in Stages.** Rather than resolve all issues at once, the entrepreneur does only enough research to justify the next action or investment. For example, an individual who has developed a new medical technology may first obtain crude estimates of market demand to determine whether it's worth seeing a patent lawyer. If the estimates and lawyer are encouraging, the individual may do more analysis to investigate the wisdom of spending money to obtain a patent. Several more iterations of analysis and action will follow before the entrepreneur prepares and circulates a formal business plan to venture capitalists.

- **Plugging Holes Quickly.** As soon as any problems or risks show up, the entrepreneur begins looking for solutions. For example, suppose that an entrepreneur sees it will be difficult to raise capital. Rather than kill the idea, he or she thinks creatively about solving the problem. Perhaps the investment can be reduced by modifying technology to use more standard equipment that can be rented instead of bought. Or under the right terms, a customer might underwrite the risk by providing a large initial order. Or expectations and goals for growth might be scaled down, and a niche market could be tackled first. Except with obviously unviable ideas that can be ruled out through elementary logic, the purpose of analysis is not to find fault with new ventures or find reasons for abandoning them. Analysis is an exercise in what to do next more than what not to do.

*An entrepreneur's willingness to act on sketchy plans and inconclusive data is often sustained by an almost arrogant self-confidence.*

- **Evangelical Investigation.** Entrepreneurs often blur the line between research and selling. As one founder recalls, "My market research consisted of taking a prototype to a trade show and seeing if I could write orders." Software industry "beta sites" provide another example of simultaneous research and selling; customers actually pay to help vendors test early versions of their software and will often place larger orders if they are satisfied with the product.

From the beginning, entrepreneurs don't just seek opinions and information, they also look for commitment from other people. Entrepreneurs treat everyone whom they talk to as a potential customer, investor, employee, or supplier, or at least as a possible source of leads down the road. Even if they don't actually ask for an order, they take the time to build enough interest

*Entrepreneurs must be smart enough to recognize mistakes and change strategies.*

and rapport so they can come back later. This simultaneous listening and selling approach may not produce truly objective market research and statistically significant results. But the resource-constrained entrepreneur doesn't have much choice in the matter. Besides, in the initial stages, the deep knowledge and support of a few is often more valuable than broad, impersonal data.

- **Smart Arrogance.** An entrepreneur's willingness to act on sketchy plans and inconclusive data is often sustained by an almost arrogant self-confidence. One successful high-tech entrepreneur likens his kind to "gamblers in a casino who know they are good at craps and are therefore likely to win. They believe: 'I'm smarter, more creative, and harder working than most people. With my unique and rare skills, I'm doing investors a favor by taking their money.'" More-over, the entrepreneur's arrogance must stand the test of adversity. Entrepreneurs must have great con-fidence in their talent and ideas to persevere as cus-tomers stay away in droves, the product doesn't work, or the business runs out of cash.

But entrepreneurs who believe they are more capable or venturesome than others must also have the smarts to recognize their mistakes and to change their strategies as events unfold. Successful ventures don't always proceed in the direction on which they initially set out. A significant proportion develop entirely new markets, products, and sources of com-petitive advantage. Therefore, although perseverance and tenacity are valuable entrepreneurial traits, they must be complemented with flexibility and a willing-ness to learn. If prospects who were expected to place orders don't, the entrepreneur should consider reworking the concept. Similarly, the entrepreneur should also be prepared to exploit opportunities that didn't figure in the initial plan.

The evolution of Silton-Bookman Systems illustrates the importance of keeping an open mind. The venture's original plan was to sell general-purpose, PC-based soft-ware for human resource development. But established competitors who already sold similar software on main-frames were beginning to develop products for PCs. So the company adopted a niche strategy and developed a training registration product. And although the founders had initially targeted small companies that couldn't afford mainframe solutions, their first customer was someone from IBM who happened to respond to an ad. Thereafter, Silton-Bookman concentrated its efforts on large companies, where they had considerable success. "The world gives you lots and lots of feedback," cofounder Phil Bookman observes. "The challenge is to take advantage of the feedback you get."

The apparently sketchy planning and haphazard evolution of many successful ventures like Silton-Bookman doesn't mean that entrepreneurs should follow a ready-fire-aim approach. Despite appearances, astute entrepreneurs do analyze and strategize extensively. They realize, however, that businesses cannot be launched like space shuttles, with every detail of the mission planned in advance. Initial analyses only provide plausible hypotheses, which must be tested and modified. Entrepreneurs should play with and explore ideas, letting their strategies evolve through a seamless process of guesswork, analysis, and action.

## Does Planning Pay?

INTERVIEWS WITH THE FOUNDERS OF 100 COMPANIES on the 1989 *Inc.* "500" list of the fastest growing companies in the United States revealed that entrepreneurs spent little effort on their initial business plan:

41% had no business plan at all.

26% had just a rudimentary, back-of-the-envelope type of plan.

5% worked up financial projections for investors.

28% wrote up a full-blown plan.

Many entrepreneurs, the interviews suggested, don't bother with well-formulated plans for good reasons. They thrive in rapidly changing industries and niches that tend to deter established companies. And under these fluid conditions, an ability to roll with the punches is much more important than careful planning.

The experiences of two *Inc.* "500" companies, Attronica Computers and Bohdan Associates, illustrate the limitations of planning in entrepreneurial ventures. Carol Sosdian and Atul Tucker, who had worked together in a large corporation, started Attronica in 1983 to retail personal computers in Washington, D.C. Carol recalls that Atul "wrote a one-paragraph business plan and brought it to me, and I turned it into a real business plan. It took about one month, and then we bantered back and forth over the next three months. We got to where we thought it might work, and then we showed it to some friends. It passed the 'friends test.'"

Heartened, Carol and Atul conducted almost two years of market research, which led them to purchase a Byte franchise for $150,000. Soon after they opened their first store, however, Byte folded. They then signed on as a franchisee of World of Computers, which also

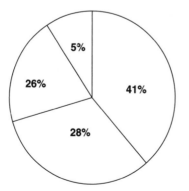

Only 28% of the entrepreneurs wrote up a full-blown plan.

folded; and in 1985, Attronica began to operate as an independent, direct dealer for AT&T's computers. This partnership clicked, and Attronica soon became one of AT&T's best dealers. Attronica also changed its customer focus from people off the street to corporate and government clients. They found large clients much more profitable because they valued Attronica's technical expertise and service.

Peter Zacharkiw founded Bohdan Associates in a Washington, D.C., suburb in the same year that Atul and Carol launched Attronica. Peter did not conduct any research, however. He was employed by Bechtel and invested in tax shelters on the side. He bought a computer for his tax shelter calculations, expecting to deduct the cost of the machine from his income. When Peter discovered that he was overdeducted for the year, he placed an ad in the *Washington Post* to sell his computer. He got over 50 responses and sold his machine for a profit. Peter figured that if he had had 50 machines, he could have sold them all and decided to begin selling computers from his home. "At first, I just wanted to earn a little extra Christmas money," he recalls. "My wife put systems together during the day, and I delivered them at night. We grew to $300,000 per month, and I was still working full-time. I made more then than I would have made the entire year at Bechtel."

Like Attronica, Bohdan evolved into serving corporate clients. "First, we sold to individuals responding to ads. But these people were working for companies, and they would tell their purchasing agents, 'Hey, I know where you can get these.' It was an all-referral business. I gave better service than anyone else. I knew the machines technically better than anyone else. I would deliver them, install them, and spend time teaching buyers how to use them." In 1985, after customers started asking for Compaq machines, Bohdan became a Compaq dealer, and the business really took off. "We're very reactive, not proactive," Peter observes. "Business comes to us, and we react. I've never had a business plan."

## Notes

1. Scott Lewis, "Microsoft Corporation," in *International Directory of Company Histories,* ed. Paula Kepos (Detroit, Michigan: St. James Press, 1992), p. 258.

2. Erik Ipsen, "Real Estate: Will Success Spoil Sam Zell?" *Institutional Investor,* April 1989, pp. 90–99.

3. See Amar Bhide, "Hustle as Strategy," HBR September–October 1986.

4. See "McKinsey & Company (A): 1956," Harvard Business School Case No. 393-066, 1992.

5. See Howard Stevenson and David Gumpert, "The Heart of Entrepreneurship," HBR March–April 1985.

Originally published in March–April 1994
Reprint 94202

# How Much Money Does Your New Venture Need?

JAMES MCNEILL STANCILL

## Executive Summary

ENTREPRENEURS SHOULD COMPILE a financial forecast
that includes three elements: an income statement, a balance sheet, and a cash flow statement. Forecasts should
look ahead five years and include three scenarios: a
most likely, a most pessimistic, and a most optimistic.

Key estimates for putting together the income statement are:

- Sales, which should be based on convincing market
  research.

- Cost of goods sold, which can involve complicated
  modeling or may be figured as a percentage of sales.

- General and administrative expenses, which must be
  based on a detailed schedule for all items.

- Selling expenses, which also require a detailed
  schedule.

Key estimates for the balance sheet are:

- Accounts receivable, which can be forecast in either of two ways.

- Inventory, which can be forecast via complex modeling or estimated.

- Debt-equity ratio, which depends on different estimates of the perceptage of debt.

These estimates allow completion of the cash flow statement, which should show monthly outcomes for several years. At first, the monthly cash flow will be negative, then increase. If it does not, more cash will be needed. Mostly the forecast will show the amount the company needs at the beginning to finance the most likely scenario.

Because forecasts aren't fool-proof, entrepreneurs should forecast alternative scenarios. In negotiating with financiers, they must be sure to obtain a commitment for the entire amount of financing necessary to get the venture started successfully and through the hardest times expected.

---

E VERY ENTREPRENEUR PLANNING A NEW VEN-
TURE faces the same dilemma: determining how much money is necessary to start the business. More often than not, entrepreneurs estimate on the low side. They may simply not allow for unexpected expenses and lower-than-predicted sales.

It is impossible to know exactly how much a new business will need during its first five years, but it is possible to come up with realistic estimates. These come from the financial forecast: the income statement, the balance sheet, and, most important, the cash flow statement.

This reading shows how to calculate the new venture's capital requirements through such financial forecasting. It also shows how financial forecasting provides the basis for determining equity investments.

Thanks to various computer spreadsheet programs, calculations associated with even the most detailed forecasting are fairly simple. What used to require days or weeks now takes only minutes or hours. Such programs enable entrepreneurs to use variables and test scenarios in ways that are impractical with conventional push-the-pencil methods. Such split-second calculating tools should not, of course, blind entrepreneurs to the logic of the numerical estimate and the cash flow model.

## Beginning the Process

Simplicity is a virtue in presenting financial statements. Show items in summary form, but reserve all the details for separate schedules or footnotes attached to the financial statements. And make certain the statements conform with generally accepted format practices; creativity is welcome in many areas of business planning but not in financial statements.

For most manufacturing and many other start-ups, the form of the income statement will be like that shown in the exhibit "Sample Income Statement." Each item has a footnote, which is included in "Notes to the financial statements." In these notes, you may refer the reader to another supporting schedule or you may simply explain the item. Each item has a separate footnote number. Having an explanation for each item is the most important aspect of an effective forecast. By explaining each item, you can defuse disputes about what value an item should have. If much uncertainty exists about an item, you can state in the footnote that the estimate is merely a guess but that the general order of magnitude is probably appropriate.

The financial forecast initially requires three estimates of sales for five years: a most likely, a most pessimistic, and a most optimistic estimate. Express this sales forecast in both number of items sold and dollars to account for factors that might affect the selling price. The sales forecasts should, of course, be accompanied by written justification of the sales estimates so that you

---

### Sample Income Statement

| | |
|---|---|
| Sales[1] | $XXX |
| Less cost of goods sold[2] | XXX |
| **Gross profit margin** | <u>XXX</u> |
| Less general and administrative expenses[3] | XXX |
| Less selling expenses[4] | XXX |
| **Operating income or loss** | <u>XXX</u> |
| Less interest expense | XXX |
| Income before taxes | XXX |
| Less income taxes[5] | XXX |
| **Net income or loss** | <u>$XXX</u> |

---

Notes:

1. The sales forecasts shown here are based on market research, details of which are provided separately.

2. See the separate cost accounting module for details of how the cost of goods was arrived at [not shown in this reading].

3. See the exhibit "General and Administrative Expenses, Year 1, the McDonald Company."

4. See the exhibit "Selling Expenses, Year 1, the McDonald Company, Most Likely Case."

5. This includes federal and corporate income taxes.

can begin to project the required financial statements—first the income statement, then the balance sheet, and finally the cash flow statement.

A pro forma five-year income statement is, of course, only tentative. It is based on the assumption that the proposed output is feasible and that the level of production can be financed.

Before putting together the income statement, the forecaster must project which assets and liabilities will support the forecast sales level. This projection leads to

---

## Sample Balance Sheet

| ASSETS | | LIABILITIES | |
|---|---|---|---|
| Cash | $XXX | Accounts payable[11] | $XXX |
| Accounts receivable[6] | XXX | Accrued taxes[5] | XXX |
| Inventory[7] | XXX | Accrued expenses[12] | XXX |
| Other assets (prepaids)[8] | XXX | Current portion of long-term debt | XXX |
| **Total current assets** | **$XXX** | | |
| | | **Total current liabilities** | **$XXX** |
| Plant, property, and equipment at cost[9] | XXX | Long-term equipment loans[13] | XXX |
| Less reserve for depreciation[10] | XXX | Equity | XXX |
| Net plant, property, and equipment | XXX | Retained earnings or loss | XXX |
| | | **Total liabilities and capital** | **$XXX** |
| **Total assets** | **$XXX** | | |

---

Notes:

5. *This includes federal and corporate income taxes.*

6. *See the exhibit "Calculation of the McDonald Company's Monthly Accounts Receivable Balance, Year 1" for the aging schedule.*

7. *For details of the finished-goods inventory, see the exhibit "Calculation of Finished-Goods Inventory, the McDonald Company."*

8. *For the changes in prepaid assets, see separate schedule [not shown in this reading].*

9. *See separate schedule [not shown in this reading].*

10. *Generally, straight-line depreciation was used for equipment.*

11. *See separate schedule for details of charges in accounts payable [not shown in this reading].*

12. *See separate schedule for details of changes in accrued expenses [not shown in this reading].*

13. *The face amount of the loans is $140,000, payable in monthly installments of $5,023 for 36 months at an interest rate of 15%.*

the balance sheet estimate. For most new ventures, the balance sheet form shown in the exhibit "Sample Balance Sheet" is appropriate.

At this preliminary stage, it is important to avoid structuring the balance sheet—and the terms of the financing—by putting in the entire amount of outside investments or loans. Unless the whole proposal is to be syndicated, leave the decision about the allocation of debt and equity to the financiers. Thus, the cash account, even if negative, becomes the balancing item on the balance sheet.

Most new ventures should do projections for five years—a monthly forecast for the first two or three years and quarterly or yearly projections for the remaining years. The time period each statement covers should be the same. That is, you shouldn't have monthly income statements and quarterly balance sheets for each period.

The monthly forecasts serve two purposes. First, they act as a form of budget, especially for general, administrative, and sales expenses. Second, they show the effect of quarterly tax payments on cash flow. The need to forecast for five years is dictated by the venture capitalist's desire to determine future earnings so as to arrive at a projected value for the business. This value, in turn, largely determines how much equity the venture capitalist will insist on for the capital investment.

## Getting to Cost of Goods Sold

To illustrate the forecasting of capital requirements, I'll use the case of the McDonald Company, which was created to manufacture a water-purification unit for maritime and other uses. A colleague and I assumed that the company would start in January of year 1, would not produce any units in the first month, but would then produce 100 units a month in February through April and 300 a month for the next three months. It would then start dropping production in anticipation of seasonally lower sales and make a total of 2,100 units for the first year. The company did enough market research to warrant the sales forecast for the most-likely scenario. We assumed a selling price of $600 per unit, resulting in sales for year 1 of $1,020,000. We forecast that sales would rise in year 2 to $3 million and in year 3 to $3,780,000, and that the company would grow 25% in years 4 and 5.

After you have made the sales forecast, the next and most important item to estimate is the cost of goods sold. In service and wholesale businesses, making this estimate is not as complicated as in manufacturing. In service and wholesale, pricing, and thus sales, will probably be a function of labor or cost of materials; and a forecast of sales in units will easily produce a forecast of cost of goods sold.

For a manufacturing venture, simply using a percentage of sales, as you might when the business is reasonably well established, could lead to some serious errors. Unfortunately, the proper way is quite laborious and complicated, for it means using a separate forecast model. For the McDonald Company, we did an elaborate cost accounting module for all three scenarios, which turned out to be extraordinarily expensive in terms of time, even though we did it on a computer.

Remembering that the cost of goods sold consists of direct labor, cost of materials, and factory overhead, we handled the cost accounting model in the following way. Starting with a section on volume data, we forecast unit sales. Next, we made a decision on production, which began two months before sales were to commence. (This decision led to an ending inventory total that rose and fell as monthly sales went up and down.) In general, average wage rates and the time needed to assemble a unit were fairly easy to forecast.

Other components of the cost accounting model were raw materials, inventory, work-in-process inventory, finished-goods inventory, total inventory, factory overhead, work-in-process flow in units, and weighted-average cost per unit.

In some cases, estimating cost of goods sold as a percentage of sales, albeit a declining percentage, may be sufficient for the purpose at hand, particularly if you consider all the other variables. For example, after we made the cost accounting model for the McDonald Company, we calculated the cost of goods sold as a percentage of sales. Beginning at 53%, the percentage declined to about 40%. If it were possible to estimate the ratio of cost of goods sold to sales for, say, six-month intervals, the results would be approximately the same as what we got through the modeling. But for the shortcut approach, remember to have the necessary facts on hand to support the assumed percentages—such as efficiency of assembly, declining cost of raw materials because of increasing purchases, and spreading the factory overhead over the growing number of units purchased.

## Key Expenses

Estimate the depreciation expenses that are assumed to be included in the cost of goods sold so that this amount can be removed when you are compiling the cash flow statement. (To calculate taxable profit or loss, you must include the depreciation expense in the income statement; you can show it as a separate item.)

General and administrative expense (G&A) is the next income statement item to forecast. Since sales are increasing over the five-year planning horizon and G&A is mostly fixed, estimating this item as a percentage of sales is inappropriate. Instead, you must forecast a detailed schedule for all the items. Although the income statement shows only the total G&A expense, a footnote can refer the reader to the detailed schedule of G&A expenses.

The list of items in the exhibit "General and Administrative Expenses, Year 1, the McDonald Company" is rep-

---

### General and Administrative Expenses, Year 1, the McDonald Company

| | Jan. | Feb. | Mar. | Apr. | May | June | Jul. |
|---|---|---|---|---|---|---|---|
| Consultant fees | $2,000 | $2,000 | $2,000 | $2,000 | $2,000 | $2,000 | $2,000 |
| Depreciation | 400 | 400 | 400 | 400 | 400 | 400 | 400 |
| Insurance | 200 | 200 | 200 | 200 | 200 | 200 | 200 |
| Legal & acct. | 500 | 500 | 500 | 500 | 500 | 500 | 500 |
| Govt. lobbying | 3,000 | 3,000 | 3,500 | 500 | 500 | 500 | 3,000 |
| Office supplies | 1,000 | 1,000 | 1,000 | 1,000 | 1,000 | 1,000 | 1,000 |
| Payroll taxes | 840 | 1,060 | 1,260 | 1,260 | 1,260 | 1,260 | 1,380 |
| Rent | 400 | 400 | 400 | 400 | 400 | 400 | 400 |
| Office salaries | 1,800 | 1,800 | 1,800 | 1,800 | 1,800 | 1,800 | 1,800 |
| Officer salaries | 3,000 | 3,000 | 3,000 | 3,000 | 3,000 | 3,000 | 3,000 |
| Telephone | 800 | 800 | 800 | 1,200 | 1,200 | 1,200 | 1,500 |
| Non-sales travel | 2,000 | 2,000 | 2,000 | 2,000 | 1,400 | 1,400 | 1,000 |
| Utilities | 100 | 100 | 100 | 100 | 100 | 100 | 100 |
| Start-up expense | 12,000 | 3,000 | 8,000 | 0 | 0 | 0 | 12,000 |
| Bad debts | 0 | 0 | 0 | 1,800 | 5,400 | 5,400 | 5,400 |
| Totals | $28,040 | $19,260 | $24,960 | $16,160 | $19,160 | $19,160 | $19,580 |

resentative of what might be included. One item deserves special attention: officer's salaries. While entrepreneurs go into business to make lots of money, seeking one's fortune in a struggling new venture is foolish. Even if the entrepreneur is providing all the necessary start-up funds, the wisdom of taking a salary comparable to what might be expected in a more mature company is questionable, to say the least. Investors do not, however, expect the entrepreneur to live on a clerk's salary. Perhaps the best advice is to start off rather low and increase the salary as profits permit. McDonald assumed it would hire a second officer after the first year, so the total was the product of two, and later more, officers' salaries.

McDonald's other G&A expenses included such calculations as payroll taxes, predetermined items like rent and insurance, and items to be negotiated, such as lobbying in the state capital. Some items were mere guesses (nonsales travel and telephone), and some catchall attempts (start-up costs).

Selling expenses can be treated the same as G&A. A company needs to develop a detailed schedule (see the exhibit "Selling Expenses, Year 1, the McDonald Company, Most Likely Case" for an example) to include the

### Selling Expenses, Year 1, the McDonald Company, Most Likely Case

|                | Jan.     | Feb.     | Mar.     | Apr.     | May      | June     | Jul.     |
|----------------|----------|----------|----------|----------|----------|----------|----------|
| Advertising    | $6,000   | $6,000   | $8,000   | $4,000   | $4,000   | $4,000   | $4,000   |
| Travel         | 3,600    | 5,800    | 7,200    | 7,200    | 7,200    | 7,200    | 7,200    |
| Salaries       | 3,600    | 5,800    | 7,800    | 7,800    | 7,800    | 7,800    | 7,800    |
| Promo supplies | 0        | 0        | 10,000   | 1,000    | 1,000    | 1,000    | 1,000    |
| Commissions    | 0        | 0        | 0        | 0        | 0        | 0        | 0        |
| Totals         | $13,200  | $17,600  | $33,000  | $20,000  | $20,000  | $20,000  | $20,000  |

items relevant to the business at hand. For McDonald Company, we included salaries for two salespeople for the first month, three for the second, and four for the fourth month on through the rest of the first year. Travel expenses for the salespersons were estimated to be equal to salaries after the first few months. Interest expense on the equipment loan for the McDonald Company was $2,333 for the first month and declined thereafter as principal was paid.

The only other forecast item on the income statement is taxes. At first, there are no taxes, but even with the tax-loss carry forward (forward for 15 years, back for 3), taxes have to be included for the second year. Include state income taxes, if any, and use the percentage to be applied to net profit before tax. Estimating state income taxes is quite simple; the complication comes in forecasting the accrued taxes for the balance sheet. Once the income forecast is complete, you can turn to the balance sheet.

## Completing the Balance Sheet

Keep the balance sheet as simple as you did the income statement. The first item on the balance sheet—cash—is the balancing item and is thus not forecast separately. Instead, it results from the computation of the cash flow statement.

Accounts receivable may be forecast in two ways, each yielding different results. The more complicated way is to estimate what percentage of this month's sales the company will collect this month (for the McDonald Company, we assumed 5%), what percentage for the next month (we assumed 50%), and what percentage for the following two months (we assumed 30% and 15%). A separate schedule is necessary (for example, see the exhibit "Calculation of the McDonald Company's Monthly Accounts Receivable Balance, Year 1").

The standard way of forecasting accounts receivable is to use a turnover ratio (equal to monthly sales times 12 divided by the turnover figure—for example, 9). Because of the seasonality of sales, you would get dramatically different accounts receivable balances if you applied a constant turnover to each month.

In the first year for McDonald, the turnovers would have been those shown in the exhibit "Turnover at the McDonald Company," Part A.

---

### Calculation of the McDonald Company's Monthly Accounts Receivable Balance, Year 1

|  | Jan. | Feb. | Mar. | Apr. | May | June |
|---|---|---|---|---|---|---|
| Beginning accounts receivable | $0 | $0 | $0 | $0 | $55,290 | $192,060 |
| Add sales (debits)[1] | 0 | 0 | 0 | 58,200 | 174,600 | 174,600 |
| Subtotal | 0 | 0 | 0 | 58,200 | 229,890 | 366,660 |
| Collections[2] |  |  |  |  |  |  |
| Month's sales (5%) | 0 | 0 | 0 | 2,910 | 8,730 | 8,730 |
| 1 month ago (50%) |  | 0 | 0 | 0 | 29,100 | 87,300 |
| 2 months ago (30%) |  |  | 0 | 0 | 0 | 17,460 |
| 3 months ago (15%) |  |  |  | 0 | 0 | 0 |
| Total collections | 0 | 0 | 0 | 2,910 | 37,830 | 113,490 |
| Ending accounts receivable | 0 | 0 | 0 | 55,290 | 192,060 | 253,170 |
| **Change in accounts receivable** | $0 | $0 | $0 | $55,290 | $136,770 | $61,110 |

Notes:
1. Assumes net of bad debts.
2. Representative collection figures assumed for years 4 and 5.

These turnovers make clear that the first procedure is advisable for monthly cash flow forecasting for a new venture, especially if sales are seasonal.

Inventory presents a more difficult problem than accounts receivable. Because of the pronounced seasonality in production and sales, using a constant turnover for cost of goods sold is not possible. For example, the inventory turnovers for the McDonald Company for the first year were as shown in the exhibit "Turnover at the McDonald Company," Part B.

While the balance sheet shows inventory as one line, three types of inventory are actually on hand at any time: raw material, work in process, and finished goods. If you are using a cost accounting model, each month will produce these three totals. But because of the complexity of this model, you may wish to estimate (perhaps *guess* is the better term) what each of these inventory components will be, total them for each month, and use that number as the amount for inventory for the balance sheet. In the case of McDonald, we estimated unit production for the first year to be as shown in the exhibit "Calculation of Finished-Goods Inventory, the McDonald Company."

---

## Turnover at the McDonald Company

**A. Turnover of accounts receivable**

|  | May | June | July | Aug. | Sept. | Oct. | Nov. | Dec. |
|---|---|---|---|---|---|---|---|---|
| Turnover | 39.1% | 11.3% | 8.5% | 5.3% | 1.7% | 6.8% | 12.6% | 12.7% |

**B. Turnover of inventory**

|  | May | June | July | Aug. | Sept. | Oct. | Nov. | Dec. |
|---|---|---|---|---|---|---|---|---|
| Turnover | 3.6% | 3.0% | 3.7% | 3.0% | 0.1% | 1.0% | 1.6% | 1.1% |

By estimating the average cost of each finished unit, you can approximate the finished-goods component of inventory. With an eye to the production schedule, you can estimate how much raw material you will require. By spreading this raw material over the other months, you can get a crude estimate of the raw material component. You estimate work in process by examining the production schedule and assuming an average cost for the units, say, when they are half completed.

Totaling these admittedly crude estimates (as in the exhibit "Estimated End-of-Month Inventory versus Actual Inventory, the McDonald Company") reveals a surprisingly close approximation of the needed inventory level required.

Other assets, which for a new venture include principally prepaid expenses, should be itemized and priced on a separate schedule and the total shown on the balance sheet. Do not show these items as a turnover or a percentage of sales.

Plant, property, and equipment must also be individually budgeted and not shown as a percentage of sales. If the vendor of the equipment or a third party offers

## Calculation of Finished-Goods Inventory, the McDonald Company

|  | Jan. | Feb. | Mar. | Apr. | May | June | July | Aug. | Sep. | Oct. | Nov. | Dec. |
|---|---|---|---|---|---|---|---|---|---|---|---|---|
| Number of units manufactured | 0 | 100 | 100 | 100 | 300 | 300 | 300 | 200 | 100 | 200 | 200 | 200 |
| Cumulative units manufactured | 0 | 100 | 200 | 300 | 600 | 900 | 1,200 | 1,400 | 1,500 | 1,700 | 1,900 | 2,100 |
| Less cumulative units sold | 0 | 0 | 0 | 100 | 400 | 700 | 1,000 | 1,200 | 1,250 | 1,350 | 1,500 | 1,700 |
| Finished-goods inventory | 0 | 100 | 200 | 200 | 200 | 200 | 200 | 200 | 250 | 350 | 400 | 400 |

financing, show it in the liabilities section of the balance sheet.

For the McDonald Company, the accounts payable amount included all raw material purchases except for the initial one and assumed payment in the following month. These purchases further assumed, of course, that once under way the business could get credit. For other companies, accounts payable might include items in addition to raw material purchases. For the McDonald Company, we put those items in a separate account—accrued expenses (not shown on the sample cash flow statement). For the accounts payable forecast, we simply let the raw materials purchased lag one month.

Accrued expenses for the McDonald Company included prepaid, selling, and G&A expenses less insurance, depreciation, and bad debts. We assumed most of these expenses would be paid in the following month and let them lag one month for balance sheet purposes. Payroll taxes we assumed would be paid quarterly.

Accrued taxes are the result of applying the tax rules to the income statement item for taxes. Taxes are payable on the fifteenth day of the fourth, sixth, ninth,

---

### Estimated End-of-Month Inventory versus Actual Inventory, the McDonald Company (in thousands of dollars, crudely estimated)

| | Jan. | Feb. | Mar. | Apr. | May | June | July | Aug. | Sep. | Oct. | Nov. | Dec. |
|---|---|---|---|---|---|---|---|---|---|---|---|---|
| Raw material | $198 | $100 | $154 | $150 | $140 | $132 | $120 | $110 | $132 | $120 | $110 | $330 |
| Work in process | 25 | 25 | 25 | 75 | 75 | 75 | 50 | 25 | 50 | 50 | 50 | 125 |
| Finished goods | 0 | 32 | 63 | 95 | 158 | 158 | 158 | 126 | 95 | 142 | 173 | 189 |
| Estimated | $223 | $157 | $242 | $320 | $373 | $365 | $328 | $261 | $277 | $312 | $333 | $644 |
| Actual | $208 | $219 | $283 | $378 | $310 | $375 | $300 | $248 | $383 | $370 | $341 | $652 |

and twelfth months, and estimates can be based on the prior year's taxes or the current year's earnings. (We used the prior year's for McDonald.)

How do you best handle the delicate problem of distinguishing between long-term debt and equity? My preference is to include in long-term debt only what I call "bring-along financing"—that is, financing that is offered almost as a matter of course on such purchases as equipment. (Real estate, too, might involve such financing, but buying land and buildings at the start of a new venture would be a strange use of precious funds. It's better to rent or lease until the business is well established.)

Structuring the debt/equity ratio of a new venture is quite acceptable if you are underwriting or syndicating the venture yourself. But if you have to go to one or two venture capital sources for the bulk of the financing, you will probably want to leave that decision to your outside investors. (I once lost the financing for a start-up venture when the institution took exception to my structuring the deal. It thought the debt/equity issue was its prerogative and rejected the deal rather than hassle over the matter.) Interest and principal payments will throw off the cash flow forecast, but you can correct this imbalance later.

In this model, the object is to forecast how much money will be needed to capitalize the venture. To avoid anticipating the decision of potential financiers, it's best not to consider how much of this to invest via debt instruments and how much by equity—common or preferred stock. When that decision is made and the capitalization known, the forecast can be revised to include this decision. An overdraft in the cash account can replace the required long-term debt and equity, at least initially.

## At Last: The Cash Flow Statement

Once you have completed the income statement and the balance sheet forecasts, you have the ingredients for the cash flow statement. Essentially a combination of the income statement and the balance sheet, it shows the changes that will occur in the cash balance.

Before considering the items on the cash flow statement, I must point out that for income statement items, the actual dollar amount is shown for the period in question. For example, if net sales for one month were $300,000, the amount would appear on the cash flow statement for that month. (See the exhibit "Sample Cash Flow Statement" for a sample cash flow statement.)

For balance sheet items, however, it is the period-to-period change that should be included in the cash flow statement, and whether the change is added or subtracted is indicated by the symbol $+\Delta$ or $-\Delta$, which should be read "plus a positive change" or "minus a positive change." Of course, if the change is negative and the symbol is $-\Delta$, then algebraically this would be minus a minus, so the amount should be added.

The cash flow statement has seven parts. The first three deal with the basic operations of the company. Part one, net operating cash inflow, includes sales from the income statement minus a positive change in accounts receivable.

Later, after the venture is reasonably well established, you may want to pledge receivables and/or inventory as collateral for a working capital loan from a bank. In that case, you would add, under $-\Delta$ accounts receivable or $+\Delta$ bank borrowing, the increase or decrease in the loan amount. Including this item in this section, even though it is a financial rather than an operating matter, pre-

## Sample Cash Flow Statement

**CASH FLOW STATEMENT FOR THE PERIOD \_\_\_\_ TO \_\_\_\_**

| | *Month* | | | |
|---|---|---|---|---|
| *Operating cash inflows* | | | | |
| + Net sales | $ | $ | $ | $ |
| + Other income | | | | |
| – Δ Accounts receivable[1] | | | | |
| **1 Net operating cash inflows** | $ | $ | $ | $ |
| *Operating cash outflows* | | | | |
| + Cost of goods sold less depreciation | $ | $ | $ | $ |
| + General and administrative expenses | | | | |
| + Selling expenses | | | | |
| + Taxes | | | | |
| – Δ Accrued taxes | | | | |
| + Δ Inventory | | | | |
| + Δ Prepaid expenses | | | | |
| – Δ Accounts payable | | | | |
| **2 Total operating cash outflows** | $ | $ | $ | $ |
| **3 Net operating cash flow (item 1 less item 2)** | $ | $ | $ | $ |
| *Priority outflows* | | | | |
| + Interest expenses | $ | $ | $ | $ |
| + Current debt repayable | | | | |
| + Lease payments (not included above) | | | | |
| **4 Total priority outflows** | $ | $ | $ | $ |
| *Discretionary outflows* | | | | |
| + Capital expenditures | $ | $ | $ | $ |
| + Research and development expenses | | | | |
| + Preferred stock dividends | | | | |
| + Common stock dividends | | | | |
| **5 Total discretionary outflows** | $ | $ | $ | $ |
| *Financial flows* | | | | |
| + Δ Debt instruments (borrowings) | $ | $ | $ | $ |
| + Δ Stock securities (equity) | | | | |
| + Δ Term loans | | | | |
| **6 Total financial flows** | $ | $ | $ | $ |
| *Net change in cash and marketable securities accounts* | | | | |
| + Net operating cash flow (item 3) | $ | $ | $ | $ |
| – Priority outflows (item 4) | | | | |
| – Discretionary outflows (item 5) | | | | |
| + Financial flows (item 6) | | | | |
| **7 Net change in cash and marketable securities** | $ | $ | $ | $ |
| *End-of-period cash balance* | $ | $ | $ | $ |

Note:
1. Δ = Period-to-period change in total dollar amount.

vents the net operating cash flow (NOCF) from being negative much of the time.

It is true that if you start out using a receivables-based credit line, you will need less venture capital to start the business. But this type of financing may make it impossible to obtain extra financing later because the company will have no collateral left to offer. It is best instead to leave receivables-based financing as a contingency financing source in case it's really needed.

Even worse would be factoring, which is the sale of the receivable. I first formed this opinion in the course of assisting with the start-up of an ophthalmic laboratory. The entrepreneur's lawyer did his best to convince us that we should sell the receivables to the company for which he was counsel. We resisted, and well we did, for when the venture got into trouble, it was able to use the receivables as another source of capital.

The second part of the cash flow statement, total operating cash outflows, includes cost of goods sold (excluding depreciation), G&A expenses, selling expenses, and taxes from the income statement. Next comes minus a positive change in accrued taxes, plus a positive change in inventory and prepaid expenses, and $-\Delta$ accounts payable. Subtract this second item, total operating cash outflows, from the first, net operating cash inflows, and the result is net operating cash flow. NOCF pinpoints how much cash was generated from the basic operations of the company. This is cash with which to grow the company.

The first use of NOCF is to pay the priority out-flows, which consist of interest expense and debt repayment. Here you would also include a large lease payment—say for the premises the company occupies—in lieu of a mortgage payment. (Small lease payments go under cost of goods sold, G&A expense, or selling expense.)

The next section, discretionary outflows, includes a ranking of four discretionary expenditures. For example, in certain businesses—toys, for example—advertising expenses might be as much as or more than R&D or capital expenditures in other businesses. Even the sequence can be different. Use whatever sequence fits your business.

If you plan to buy equipment and have the manufacturer or other third party finance a portion of the price, you would, looking at the exhibit "Sample Cash Flow Statement," record the transaction as follows: show the total price of the equipment in the "start" column for capital expenditures, the amount of the note in the start column as a debt instrument in the financial flows section, and periodic payments in their respective time period columns as priority outflow—interest expense and debt repayment.

In the initial financial cash flow forecast for the new venture, I suggest that no entry be made in the financial flows section except the bring-along financing I referred to previously.

The punch line of the cash flow statement is part seven, net change in cash and marketable securities. This is defined as part three (NOCF) minus part four (total priority outflows) minus part five (total discretionary outflows) plus or minus part six (total financial flows). For convenience, the end-of-period cash balance (the same as the balance sheet amount) is shown at the very bottom of the cash flow statement.

Since cash is the balancing item in the financial forecast, part seven would normally be negative for at least the first few months. This information helps answer the question on every entrepreneur's mind.

## How Much Cash is Needed?

The cash flow projection gives a reasonable estimate of the amount of cash needed to start the venture.

If net change in cash is –$57,833 in a month (as it was in February of Year 1 for the McDonald Company), the business would have zero dollars at the end of the month if it started that month with $57,833 in its cash (checking) account. Not all monthly changes are negative, but if we algebraically add these changes to net change in cash, a running cash balance emerges for the end of the month.

The exhibit "Cash Flow Statement for the McDonald Company, Year 1; Jan.–Mar., Year 2" shows a portion of the most likely scenario for the first two years of the cash flow statement for the McDonald Company. This projected negative cash balance keeps increasing until it reaches a maximum decrease in January of year 2 of –$846,063. From this time on, the cumulative cash balance rises, becomes a positive balance briefly in December of year 2, and falls back to a negative number for several more months until June of year 3, when it becomes positive consistently. This means that the company needs $846,063 in its bank account at the start to finance the most likely scenario of the financial forecast.

But what if the company does not meet these forecasts exactly? Surely it won't!

The solution is to forecast two other scenarios—a most pessimistic and a most optimistic situation. These forecasts are not as much trouble as they may seem since a number of items are the same for all these scenarios.

While these forecasts are not shown here, we did them for the McDonald Company and noted the largest decrease in the cash balance for each scenario. For the most optimistic scenario, the maximum negative cash balance was $1,052,289 (occurring in April of year 2). For

### Cash Flow Statement for the McDonald Company, Year 1; Jan.–Mar., Year 2

|  | Jan. | Feb. | Mar. | Apr. | May | June |
|---|---|---|---|---|---|---|
| Operating cash inflows |  |  |  |  |  |  |
| + Net sales | $0 | $0 | $0 | $60,000 | $180,000 | $180,000 |
| – Change in accounts receivable | 0 | 0 | 0 | 55,290 | 136,770 | 61,110 |
| (1) Net operating cash inflows | 0 | 0 | 0 | 4,710 | 43,230 | 118,890 |
| Operating cash outflows |  |  |  |  |  |  |
| + COGS (less depreciation) | 0 | 0 | 0 | 32,013 | 94,165 | 93,227 |
| + G & A expense (less depreciation) | 27,640 | 18,860 | 24,560 | 15,760 | 18,760 | 18,760 |
| + Selling expenses | 13,200 | 17,600 | 33,000 | 20,000 | 20,000 | 20,000 |
| + Taxes | 0 | 0 | 0 | 0 | 0 | 0 |
| – Change in accrued taxes | 0 | 0 | 0 | 0 | 0 | 0 |
| + Change in inventory | 208,430 | 10,430 | 164,430 | (5,723) | (67,875) | 65,063 |
| + Change in prepaid expenses | 2,200 | (200) | (200) | (200) | (200) | (200) |
| – Change in accounts payable | 43,040 | (5,940) | 173,000 | (176,340) | 660 | 129,480 |
| (2) Net operating cash outflows | 208,430 | 52,630 | 48,790 | 238,190 | 64,190 | 67,370 |
| (3) Net operating cash flow | (208,430) | (52,630) | (48,790) | (233,480) | (20,960) | 51,520 |
| Priority outflows |  |  |  |  |  |  |
| + Interest expenses | 2,333 | 2,286 | 2,237 | 2,187 | 2,137 | 2,086 |
| + Current debt repayable | 2,870 | 2,917 | 2,966 | 3,015 | 3,066 | 3,117 |
| (4) Total priority outflows | 5,203 | 5,203 | 5,203 | 5,202 | 5,203 | 5,203 |

the most pessimistic scenario, the comparable number for the first two years was $859,756 (occurring in April of year 2). It's not really surprising that the most optimistic scenario required more cash than the most pessimistic, as generating more sales meant heightening working capital requirements, especially accounts receivable and inventory.

| July | Aug. | Sept. | Oct. | Nov. | Dec. | Jan. | Feb. | Mar. |
|---|---|---|---|---|---|---|---|---|
| $180,000 | $120,000 | $30,000 | $60,000 | $90,000 | $120,000 | $180,000 | $300,000 | $420,000 |
| 17,460 | (55,290) | (109,125) | (20,370) | 27,645 | 45,105 | 74,460 | 143,085 | 173,640 |
| 162,540 | 175,290 | 139,125 | 80,370 | 62,355 | 74,895 | 105,540 | 156,915 | 246,360 |
| 93,077 | 62,498 | 15,629 | 31,245 | 46,845 | 62,074 | 92,284 | 153,179 | 213,731 |
| 19,180 | 17,380 | 14,680 | 15,580 | 16,480 | 17,380 | 29,610 | 32,010 | 34,410 |
| 20,000 | 20,000 | 20,000 | 20,000 | 20,000 | 20,000 | 41,000 | 43,400 | 45,800 |
| 0 | 0 | 0 | 0 | 0 | 0 | 9,302 | 27,426 | 49,309 |
| 0 | 0 | 0 | 0 | 0 | 0 | 9,302 | 27,426 | 49,309 |
| (74,717) | (52,068) | 134,731 | (12,885) | (28,485) | 310,076 | (50,134) | (111,029) | 188,349 |
| (200) | (200) | (200) | (200) | (200) | (200) | 2,750 | (250) | (250) |
| (130,320) | 1,380 | 129,240 | (130,620) | 1,380 | 327,040 | (292,440) | 1,960 | 349,280 |
| 187,660 | 46,230 | 55,600 | 184,360 | 53,260 | 82,090 | 407,950 | 115,350 | 132,760 |
| (25,120) | 129,060 | 83,525 | (103,990) | 9,095 | (7,195) | (302,410) | 41,565 | 113,600 |
| 2,034 | 1,981 | 1,928 | 1,873 | 1,818 | 1,761 | 1,704 | 1,645 | 1,586 |
| 3,169 | 3,222 | 3,275 | 3,330 | 3,385 | 3,442 | 3,499 | 3,557 | 3,617 |
| 5,203 | 5,203 | 5,203 | 5,203 | 5,203 | 5,203 | 5,203 | 5,203 | 5,203 |

If you take the larger difference between the maximum negative cash balance for the most likely scenario and either the most optimistic or the most pessimistic situation, you get an estimate of our contingency factor. In this case, the most pessimistic is only $13,693 more

---

### Cash Flow Statement for the McDonald Company, Year 1; Jan.–Mar., Year 2 (continued)

| | Jan. | Feb. | Mar. | Apr. | May | June |
|---|---|---|---|---|---|---|
| Discretionary outflows + Capital expenditures | 200,000 | 0 | 0 | 0 | 0 | 0 |
| (5) Total discretionary outflows | 200,000 | 0 | 0 | 0 | 0 | 0 |
| Financial flows + Debt instruments (borrowings) | 140,000 | 0 | 0 | 0 | 0 | 0 |
| (6) Total financial flows | 140,000 | 0 | 0 | 0 | 0 | 0 |
| Net change in cash and marketable securities + Net operating cash flow (item 3) | (208,430) | (52,630) | (48,790) | (233,480) | (20,960) | 51,520 |
| – Priority outflows (item 4) | 5,203 | 5,203 | 5,203 | 5,202 | 5,203 | 5,203 |
| – Discretionary outflows (item 5) | 200,000 | 0 | 0 | 0 | 0 | 0 |
| + Financial flows (item 6) | 140,000 | 0 | 0 | 0 | 0 | 0 |
| (7) Net change in cash and marketable securities | ($273,633) | ($57,833) | ($53,993) | ($238,682) | ($26,163) | $46,317 |
| Projected ending cash balance | ($273,633) | ($331,466) | ($385,459) | ($624,141) | ($650,304)[1] | ($603,987) |

Note:
1. *Maximum negative cash balance.*

than the most likely scenario number, but the difference for the most optimistic projection is $194,846.

Surely, if you listed the capital required as $846,063 plus a contingency reserve of $194,846, your figures would have specious accuracy, which would not speak

| July | Aug. | Sept. | Oct. | Nov. | Dec. | Jan. | Feb. | Mar. |
|---|---|---|---|---|---|---|---|---|
| 0 | 0 | 0 | 0 | 0 | 0 | 0 | 0 | 0 |
| 0 | 0 | 0 | 0 | 0 | 0 | 0 | 0 | 0 |
| 0 | 0 | 0 | 0 | 0 | 0 | 0 | 0 | 0 |
| 0 | 0 | 0 | 0 | 0 | 0 | 0 | 0 | 0 |
| (25,120) | 129,060 | 83,525 | (103,990) | 9,095 | (7,195) | (302,410) | 41,565 | 113,600 |
| 5,203 | 5,203 | 5,203 | 5,203 | 5,203 | 5,203 | 5,203 | 5,202 | 5,203 |
| 0 | 0 | 0 | 0 | 0 | 0 | 0 | 0 | 0 |
| 0 | 0 | 0 | 0 | 0 | 0 | 0 | 0 | 0 |
| ($30,323) | $123,857 | $78,322 | ($109,193) | $3,892 | ($12,398) | ($307,613) | $36,363 | $108,397 |
| ($634,310) | ($510,453) | ($432,131) | ($541,324) | ($537,432) | ($549,830) | ($857,443) | ($821,080) | ($712,683) |

well for the forecaster. So round off the numbers and state that the business needs capital of $850,000 plus a contingency amount of $200,000, or a total of $1,050,000.

What if the entrepreneurs perceive that their track record will not support a request for the amount needed to finance the venture? They can go back to the income statement and balance sheet and make adjustments that might save money. Perhaps scaling back the sales forecast even more than the most pessimistic estimate might help. A company could save on working capital or buy used machinery instead of new or could subcontract production until the business was healthy. Whatever the alternatives, you can use the same model.

Now a potential venture capitalist might examine these forecasts and say, "Fine, but you don't need all this money now, at the start. Let's put up some of the required capital, and when you need the rest, ask for it."

Such a directive can be the kiss of death for a new venture because when the entrepreneur calls for more money, the venture capitalist can well say, "Sorry, but my funds are tied up right now. You'll have to wait awhile." (This was the response the first start-up venture on which I worked got. As a result, I formed my first law of entrepreneurship: if you want to fly to financial paradise, have enough gas to make the trip, as there are no service stations along the way!)

If the business attempts to raise venture capital once it has started and before it gets to a positive cash flow position (ready for second-stage financing), all it will have to show is a trail of red ink on its financial statements. True, the new business does not need all the required cash on day 1, but the cash should be available when needed.

One way to ensure that funds will be available is to arrange with a bank for a letter of credit. Then, if the venture capital source is temporarily short of funds, the bank can advance the funds based on the venture capitalist's credit.

The process for determining the capital requirements for a new venture really is not mysterious, only a bit complicated. The key to this determination (and to financial forecasting in general) is the cash flow statement. A two-step financial forecast is advisable, one to summarize the data and two to support the data with details in footnotes and schedules.

The cash flow statement is at the heart of the answer to the question, How much cash is needed to finance the venture? The negative cash balance line on the most likely scenario provides an estimate of the required venture capital. You can calculate the contingency amount of venture capital by comparing the maximum decreases in cash balance for the other two scenarios.

**Originally published in May–June 1986**
**Reprint 86314**

# Milestones for Successful Venture Planning

ZENAS BLOCK AND

IAN C. MACMILLAN

## Executive Summary

ENTREPRENEURS DRAW UP BUSINESS PLANS for new
ventures to make various marketing, pricing, financial,
and other projections. More often than not, though, their
estimates bear little relationship to reality. These authors
argue that planning for new enterprises differs funda-
mentally from planning for existing companies, given the
inherent instability of start-ups.

How can managers launching new ventures plan
effectively for the many unknowns they will encounter?
Identifying milestones over the project's life enables
planners to both learn from experience about the enterprise's viability and make adjustments in strategy and
goals as necessary.

The authors describe ten typical milestones that new
businesses pass, including concept and product testing,
first financing, market testing, production start-up, and

117

competitive reactions. At each stage, executives must match their assumptions with actual outcomes and determine whether and how to proceed to the next milestone.

---

Starting a new business is essentially an experiment. Implicit in the experiment are a number of hypotheses (commonly called assumptions) that can be tested only by experience. The entrepreneur launches the enterprise and works to establish it while simultaneously validating or invalidating the assumptions. Because some will be dead wrong and others partially wrong, an important goal of the business plan must be to continually produce and build on new knowledge. Managers must justify moving to each new stage or milestone in the plan on the basis of information learned in the previous stage.

Learning in an evolutionary way is valuable not only for venture managers but also for investors, senior corporate managers, and directors. It can help them make informed decisions about whether to fund each stage, as indications of the business's potential unfold. They can use our milestone approach to measure management performance by examining what has been learned and how effectively the venture planners have modified plans to respond to new information—rather than using projections versus performance as the measure.

Milestone planning is hardly new. Traditionally, though, such forethought relies on predetermined dates set for reviews or project completions. The problem with date milestones is that they are totally unreliable for new ventures. Therefore, we suggest that managers make financing decisions instead as events are completed, using what they have just learned to make go, no-go, or redirection decisions. Obviously, new enterprises may need some deadlines and constraints. For instance, a recent proposal for a health and indoor tennis center included a completion date that would allow the club to open for the coming winter season. Every milestone was linked to meeting this deadline.

For most ventures, however, significant events—not dates—should determine milestones. The only hard dates in the plan should be externally imposed, for example, by factors like contract agreements or competitive pressures.

This approach to milestone planning has three advantages for enterprises.

1. It helps avoid costly mistiming errors.

2. It gives logical and practical milestones for learning and for reevaluating the entire venture.

3. It offers a methodology for "replanning" based on a growing body of ever-harder information.

## Writing the Plan

To give an event milestone maximum learning value, the business plan must define the event's completion so that managers can test any assumptions they make. For example, a plan would not read: "Milestone—completion of product development." A better, more specific statement would be:

*Milestone—completion of product development. Completion of a prototype machine that costs no more than*

*$150,000; that can be manufactured for a direct cost of
$12,000; that can produce 40 widgets per minute at 30
cents per widget; that the FCC will approve; and that
high school graduates can operate with three days of
training.*

As planners reach each milestone, they can compare
results with the detailed specifications to ascertain
whether their original assumptions still hold. Then they
can use their experience to make decisions about the
next steps.

As an example, suppose you are managing the project
we have just described and you learn after completion of
product development that the assumptions appear well
founded, except that the direct cost will be $30,000
instead of $12,000. You know that you need to find out
how you can change the price. Is there still a market at
another price? Do you continue the project, redirect it,
or abort it? How does the new target market differ from
the one you originally projected? Does the prototype
have any other features—negative or positive—you had
not anticipated? How will you go about changing your
plan? What will the changes teach you?

Few entrepreneurs use such planning for their new
ventures, explicitly mapping out a sequence of events.
More common are the horrifying consequences of not
planning thoroughly: the attendant mistimings, heightened cash-flow "burn rates," and the accumulation of
losses.

Obviously, all enterprises are different, and while
every event in a product's history can teach something,
our experience suggests several important milestones
that are likely to be most significant. We describe
them in this reading, and for each important event, we

ask appropriate questions and offer lessons based on actual cases.

## MILESTONE 1. COMPLETION OF CONCEPT AND PRODUCT TESTING

This stage has a very low cost relative to future steps and precedes complete product development; indeed, it often comes before any product development at all. This phase's purpose is to determine whether to proceed with any further development. At this point, planners consider whether a real market need exists for the product as they have conceived it or the model they have developed, or whether it has a potentially fatal flaw. At this milestone, entrepreneurs may have discovered a different opportunity as the result of testing their original concept and changing it.

The concept testing challenges assumptions made about desired product characteristics, target markets, pricing range, and perception of need. Planners need to ask themselves the following questions:

- Have we confirmed that an opportunity exists with sufficient upside gain to warrant the necessary risks and costs?

- What has this test taught us that modifies our assumptions and therefore, possibly, product-development objectives and target markets?

Concept and product model testing are probably the least expensive ways of avoiding costly failure if planners link product-development decisions to results. While some actual product development, production, and test marketing may appear cheap enough to warrant eliminating this stage, it has tremendous value as a safeguard against self-delusion and as a source of alternative-opportunity identification in every situation.

For example, long before starting development work, entrepreneurs in a word processor venture in the 1970s identified through interviews with potential users highly desirable characteristics for the processor. They then looked at important target markets with special programming needs in law firms and government agencies. Long before they initiated expensive microprogramming efforts, the founders radically revised the initial product concept, based on the research results, to be a software product rather than a combined hardware-software product.

## MILESTONE 2. COMPLETION OF PROTOTYPE

Entrepreneurs can obtain much useful information from carefully analyzing prototype development. They must look carefully at what caused road-blocks and disappointments and how they overcame them; the seeds of significant, hidden opportunities lie in the creative solutions to these frustrations.

For example, the software programmer in one venture to develop a specialized, interactive information retrieval service eventually had to work out some radically new programming procedures to overcome a serious data-searching bottleneck. When the entrepreneurs looked for lessons in the situation, they realized they had an important invention on their hands and they patented it. The invention's profit potential is ten times greater than that of the original business and was developed at a fraction of the cost.

To apply lessons from prototype completion, entrepreneurs must answer the following questions:

- What assumptions did we make about development time and costs and how have they changed? Why?

- What impact have those changes had on our plans and timing with respect to new hires, plant construction, marketing, and so forth?

- How do they affect financial needs and timing?

- What have we learned about labor, material, and equipment availability and costs and how does this affect our pricing plans?

- Do our observations and assumptions about our target markets still hold? If not, how have they changed, and how will the changes affect our plans—objectives, timing, and resource utilization—for each succeeding event?

- Do the product's characteristics fit with the original concept and plan? Does this create any new opportunities? How should we modify our actions as a consequence?

- Are our assumptions regarding significant competitors and competitive product characteristics still valid?

- How should we revise our investment requirements?

- Are our projections about important suppliers and service distributors still valid?

If planners expect product-development time to be lengthy, they may find it useful to divide development activities into submilestones for review.

## MILESTONE 3. FIRST FINANCING

Whether the first outside financing is for seed money to test the concept's potential, start-up financing for product development and market testing, or first-stage financing to initiate manufacturing or sales, the entrepreneur must understand how investors perceive the venture.

Businesses must compete in the capital as well as product markets to survive. Entrepreneurs should view securing financing as an opportunity to learn about their ventures' acceptable financial and expense structure in view of the highly competitive financial market.

For example, a publisher seeking funds for a new magazine soon learned that investors objected to her plan because she had budgeted for the purchase of a large piece of capital equipment. In a revised plan, she budgeted for leasing the equipment at conventional rates; once again she encountered resistance. Eventually, she persuaded a supplier to lend her the equipment for the first nine months of operations. This favorable assist to cash-flow projections, along with her determination, enabled her to secure the funding she needed. What was important in this case was that she treated each rejection as an opportunity to ask why the plan had been turned down, and she learned what investors considered to be an acceptable financial structure.

## MILESTONE 4. COMPLETION OF INITIAL PLANT TESTS

Entrepreneurs should use plant tests (or pilot operation for a service venture) to challenge or change their assumption and to produce information about the following:

- Material suitability and costs

- Processing costs and skills

- Investment prerequisites

- Training needs for production personnel, reject percentages and costs, and quality control requirements

- Material uniformity from suppliers

- Processing specifications, run time, and maintenance

Early data about these factors will improve performance and cost estimates during full-scale operations. In one case, entrepreneurs who were pilot testing a new process to be licensed for the manufacture of a frozen food product aimed at the traditional market for such products—the food-service market—discovered that the product was physically more durable than anyone had thought it would be. By making a point of asking themselves what new opportunity this difference created, the founders identified the possibility of consumer marketing. Because the product was robust enough, they could automatically produce it in small packages and give it high product visibility—something that had never been achieved before in this product category. The planners had assumed that the new product, like the old, would be fragile and would require exorbitantly expensive manual packaging. Company executives revised the marketing plan to include consumer as well as food-service marketing.

Fortunately, the executives had also decided not to enter any licensing agreements until they had learned all they could from the pilot studies. Now they could raise projected royalties without potential clients accusing them of reneging on prior agreements.

## MILESTONE 5. MARKET TESTING

The first truly demanding challenges of the venture's basic market assumptions occur at this milestone. The questions managers ask themselves now are:

- Have customers demonstrated that they'll buy the product? Why are they buying it? Why are they not buying it?

- Is it really different from and superior to the competition?

- Are the pricing assumptions still valid, considering emerging information about costs?

- Does the product perform well in varying field applications? Where do the problems lie and why?

- How should we modify estimates of achievable market share and size and target markets?

- Are our servicing-requirement assumptions accurate?

- What impact does this information have on plans and timing?

A group of people who had developed a new electronic device for amateur band musicians decided they could build a worthwhile small business. The first step was to produce a few hundred units for market testing. The entrepreneurs decided to make no commitment to fixed costs until they had learned from market tests at what volumes the product would sell. So they subcontracted all tasks and proceeded to test market with virtually no overhead. Test market results showed the business potential to be marginal, and the inventors dropped the project with a negligible loss.

## MILESTONE 6. PRODUCTION START-UP

The first successful production run tests the revised assumptions generated from pilot operations. The first runs are likely to reveal a host of problems that need solving. Most important, project planners will learn the true costs of producing a steady flow of the product and of meeting the quality requirements. Unfortunately, entrepreneurs consistently miscalculate the time this process takes and its impact on the timing for future events—especially plans for expanding the marketing effort and financing requirements.

Selling and making delivery commitments in anticipation of plan production can lead to extreme pressure to get the product out. Attempting to squeeze product out of a plant that is running into start-up problems can result in compromises in product quality along with production at enormous rejection rates, both of which give rise to customer dissatisfaction and waste huge amounts of resources. This vicious circle can destroy a new venture.

In the start-up of a baked-food business, a new plant scaled up from a pilot operation ran into quality problems from trying to produce too much too soon. Because the owners had already made significant delivery commitments to customers, many of whom had in turn employed sales forces to sell the product, the new business found itself operating at full scale with rejects at 20 times the planned level. The owners needed months to solve the problems and years to recover from the losses.

Planners can best manage production start-ups by making up a separate critical-path milestone plan for them and by providing for inventory accumulation before shipments begin.

## MILESTONE 7. BELLWETHER SALE

In the industrial market, this is the first substantial sale to an expected major account. In the consumer business, this is the first important sale to a significant distributor. Achieving this sale is likely to give the new business a big push forward; failure to achieve it can become a stumbling block to sales growth. Entrepreneurs learn the following from this milestone.

- How their product compares with the competition in the real world rather than on a limited test basis.

- Whether the product is functional.

- Whether to continue or alter the initial selling method.

- Information about service requirements on a continuing basis.

- Additional data regarding quality controls and specifications.

Ideally, the bellwether sale will be to an important prospect who has been in contact with the owners during the entire development of the new business and whose needs the owners have considered along the way. New opportunities may present themselves as well.

Federal Express's experience with IBM as an early large customer illustrates the learning opportunities this milestone offers. Instead of congratulating itself on its good fortune, Federal Express investigated why IBM was so strong a customer and learned that the company was using its service to reduce inventories of very expensive parts that IBM service bureaus held to support customer service. Federal Express then modified its marketing effort and targeted a significant portion of its promotion on the particular needs of its industrial customers rather than only promoting package delivery service. The company thus rapidly identified and secured a much larger industrial business than it had expected.

## MILESTONE 8. FIRST COMPETITIVE ACTION

It is obviously impossible for entrepreneurs to know in advance how competitors will respond to a new product or service. It is possible, however, to plan alternative responses to possible moves and study these moves to learn what rivals' true competitive position is.

Consider the case of an instrument company that in early 1984 developed a highly innovative microprocesor-based device. Its entire marketing campaign depended on how close a significant competitor was to coming out with an equivalent product. The top executives reasoned that if the competitor were close, the response to the new product would be to cut the prices of its existing products to reduce inventories. On the other hand, the competitor would probably first attempt to defend share by increasing its sales promotion, advertising, and other marketing efforts if it were not ready with a similar new product. When the competition did not cut prices, the instrument company moved aggressively into the market, and by late 1984 it still had the market to itself.

In another instance, a leading travel wholesaler introduced a series of tours to the Middle East but hoped to discourage its biggest competitor's standard follow-the-leader reaction. The wholesaler deliberately held off from its largest advertising and promotion activities until the competitor acted. The wholesaler figured that if the competitor entered the market in a tentative manner by offering only one or two tours, that would signify only half-hearted commitment. If it entered on a grander scale, it meant business. When the competitor offered only one tour, the wholesaler responded with a blockbuster marketing campaign, which scared the competition away.

## MILESTONE 9. FIRST REDESIGN OR REDIRECTION

Entrepreneurs may discover at any point on the milestone path a need to redesign the product or alter the target market. This redirection may recast prospects for the entire venture or, at the other extreme, create whole new areas of opportunity by defining follow-on product or market needs. At this point, entrepreneurs learn the differences between what they have offered and what the market needs.

The redesign or redirection decision is a time for reexamining all the basic assumptions concerning market size, segments, investment requirements, pricing, and financing (both needs and availability). A dramatic example is the design and marketing of Apple Computer's Lisa to combat the IBM PC with enhanced features and capability. Although greatly admired for its technical aspects, Lisa sales lagged, and Apple discontinued it. The company did notice, however, a potential market in the personal computer arena for many of Lisa's features. Apple incorporated several of them into its Macintosh at a much lower price and reached a mass market.

Another case involves Thermo-Fax, which failed when 3M introduced it for researchers in copying library documents. The company redesigned the product for the office market and it became highly profitable.

## MILESTONE 10. FIRST SIGNIFICANT PRICE CHANGE

New venture planners must base all their pro forma activities on assumptions regarding prices, costs, and competition, but the true value of a product or service is difficult to know until the company launches it in a competitive environment. Changes in competition, technology, and costs may force a large price revision, which, because of its direct effect on the bottom line, can make this milestone the most important in determining whether to abandon a project or redirect it. Entrepreneurs need to ask themselves at this stage:

- Will the price change be permanent or temporary?

- Is the business viable if this change is permanent?

- If not, what can we do to restructure fixed and variable costs to make it viable?

- Can we isolate the price change to a particular market segment?

In one case, the managers of an electronics business wanted to supply digital switching gear to the telecommunications field, but they encountered strong price resistance from telecommunications companies when they offered the equipment for sale as a unit. The price assumptions had been wrong because an insufficient incentive existed for replacing the existing product. Management offered to install the equipment and charge on a per usage basis but still had no success. Their price assumptions were still wrong because the new charge would be too high for the companies' clients. Finally, management unbundled the services and offered standard switching at a low per usage cost for the direct customers and specialized switching options (such as automatic disaster or other emergency signals) for the customers' clients on a monthly rental basis. This approach succeeded.

## Milestones, Millstones, or Tombstones?

Milestone reviews are pointless unless managers use them for making decisions. The decisions help planners determine what they can do to ensure success or reduce the cost of failure.

Each new venture has its own set of milestones. Descriptions of these important events should include a statement of the significant questions that managers need to ask to test their assumptions at each stage. Such a design forces planners to learn as well as to replan on the basis of what they have learned. The milestone approach satisfies the dual need for planning and flexibility and makes obvious the hazards of neglecting linkages between certain events.

Decision choices at each milestone are not limited to either pouring more money in to make the highly improbable occur or aborting the project altogether. Equally feasible possibilities include slowing down, speeding up, trying something to learn more, redirecting, changing scale, or postponing or resequencing certain actions. The point is that milestone planning takes entrepreneurs at the lowest possible cost to the next important stage, where they can make informed decisions rather than blunder along adhering to a fixed plan that out of ignorance they have based on faulty projections.

In summary, we recommend that new venture managers adopt the following procedure when developing a business plan:

1. Identify the most important events or actions that must occur to achieve your objectives.

2. Determine which events are prerequisites to others, that is, the necessary sequential links between events.

3. Develop a critical-path milestone chart that graphically displays the sequence.

4. Identify the significant assumptions on which the venture's success depends.

5. Ask if an event on the milestone chart will test each assumption. If not, design such a step and insert it. Specify what information will replace the assumption and how you will obtain it.

6. As each event occurs and replaces assumptions with information, review the planned future events. Where necessary, change their sequence and nature. Evaluate the business based on evolving and changing projections. Ask yourself along the way: Do the upside gain, downside risk, and feasibility assessment still justify moving ahead?

7. Establish a review schedule that relates to event completion as well as time factors. Evaluate performance based on what you have learned and what you can apply.

8. Rather than argue about whether results met projections, design financing rewards—and resource allocations and rewards—based on the results achieved.

**Originally published in September–October 1985**
**Reprint 85503**

# Strategy vs. Tactics from a Venture Capitalist

**ARTHUR ROCK**

## Executive Summary

ONE OF AMERICA'S LEADING VENTURE CAPITALISTS—
he helped finance Fairchild Semiconductor, Teledyne,
Apple, and other companies—discusses what he believes
most important for entrepreneurs to create successful,
thriving enterprises. some of Arthur Rock's insights,
gleaned from 30 years of evaluating business proposals, include:

- "Strategy is easy, but tactics are hard." The key to
  turning a good idea into a good business comes in
  day-to-day management of the company. For that
  reason, Rock says, he doesn't evaluate financial projections in business plans. He looks at the people—
  particularly the financial people—involved with any
  business start-up.

- "There's a thin line between refusing to accept criticism and sticking to your guns." Entrepreneurs must

135

be brutally honest with themselves, accepting bad news and staying on top of disappointing developments. At the same time, they must believe in their ideas.

- "A great idea won't make it without great management." Entrepreneurial companies go through three stages of growth; by the time the company becomes a large enterprise, the founder may not be the right person to run it. The best entrepreneurs understand how vital good management is to their company—and if they can't provide it themselves, they look outside and bring the right person in.

- "An entrepreneur without managerial savvy is just another promoter." There isn't one style that all entrepreneurs have. What is important, though, is to *have* a style—one that will lead people. The best entrepreneurs are also skilled managers who can be tough-minded with themselves and their team, can say "no," and ideally, are well versed in the technology on which the company is based.

---

$A$s a venture capitalist, I am often asked for my views on why some entrepreneurs succeed and others fail. Obviously, there are no cut-and-dried answers to that question. Still, a few general observations about how I evaluate new businesses should shed some light on what I think it takes to make an entrepreneurial venture thrive and grow.

Over the past 30 years, I estimate that I've looked at an average of one business plan per day, or about 300 a year, in addition to the large numbers of phone calls and business plans that simply are not appropriate. Of the 300 likely plans, I may invest in only one or two a year; and even among those carefully chosen few, I'd say that a good half fail to perform up to expectations. The problem with those companies (and with the ventures I choose *not* to take part in) is rarely one of strategy. Good ideas and good products are a dime a dozen. Good execution and good management—in a word, good *people*—are rare.

To put it another way, strategy is easy, but tactics— the day-to-day and month-to-month decisions required to manage a business—are hard. That's why I generally pay more attention to the people who prepare a business plan than to the proposal itself.

Another venture capitalist I know says, somewhat in jest, that the first thing he looks at in a business plan is the financial projections. Frankly, how anyone can figure out what sales and earnings and returns are going to be five years from now is beyond me. The first place I look is the résumés, usually found at the back. To me, they are the essence of any plan. (Maybe no one reads the middle section!)

I see the plan as really an opportunity to evaluate the people. If I like what I see in there, I try to find out more by sitting down and talking with the would-be entrepreneurs. I usually spend a long time on this. (Unless their first question is "How much money am I going to get?" Then the interview is very short.) I don't talk much during these meetings; I'm there to listen. I want to hear what they've got to say and see how they think.

Some of the questions I ask have little to do directly with the particular business under discussion: Whom do they know, and whom do they admire? What's their track record? What mistakes have they made in the past, and what have they learned from them? What is their attitude toward me as a potential investor—do they view me as a partner or as a necessary evil? I also ask specific questions about the kind of company they want to develop—say, whom do they plan to recruit, and how are they going to do it?

I am especially interested in what kind of financial people they intend to recruit. So many entrepreneurial companies make mistakes in the accounting end of the business. Many start shipping products before confirming that the orders are good, or that the customers will take the product, or that the accounts are collectible. Such endeavors are more concerned about making a short-term sales quota than about maximizing the long-term revenue stream.

Granted, the pressure on new businesses to make sales quotas is strong. And that's precisely why the company needs a very, very tough accounting department. Otherwise, it will get into trouble. I always ask what kind of chief financial officer the entrepreneurs plan to bring on board. If they understand the need for someone who will scrutinize the operation closely and impose appropriate controls, they are more likely to be able to translate their strategy into a going concern.

This may go without saying, but I also look at a person's motivation, commitment, and energy. Hard work alone doesn't bring success, of course, but all the effective entrepreneurs I've known have worked long, hard hours. And there's something more than the number of hours: the intensity of the hours. I think of two software entrepreneurs I know who are going at 110 miles per hour, 18 hours per day, 7 days a week. And they have instilled their intensity and their belief in the business in all the people who work for them.

Belief in the business, clearly, is critical. If you're going to succeed, you must have a burning desire to develop your idea; you must believe so firmly in the idea that everything else pales in comparison. I usually can tell the difference between people who have that fire in their stomachs and those who see their ideas primarily as a way to get rich. Far too many people are interested in building a financial empire instead of a great company.

I want to build great companies. That's how I get my kicks. I look for people who want the same thing.

At a presentation I gave recently, the audience's questions were all along the same lines: "What are the secrets to writing a business plan?" "How do I get in touch with venture capitalists?" "What percentage of the equity do I have to give to them?" No one asked me how to build a business! And here's a question that both amused me and bothered me: "How do I get rid of the venture capitalists after they've made their investment?"

I'm looking for entrepreneurs who ask, "How can I make this business a success?"—not "How do I make a fortune?" And I prefer someone who *wants* me to play a role in the enterprise's decision making. Obviously, when they come to me entrepreneurs are interested in getting my money. Many have the attitude, "Uh oh, is this guy going to want to come to staff meetings and open his big mouth?" But they should realize that I can be a resource for them in more ways than one. I've been around for a long time; there just aren't many business problems that I haven't seen before. And most entrepreneurs can use all the help they can get in developing and implementing the tactics that will make them successful in the long run.

When I talk to entrepreneurs, I'm evaluating not only their motivation but also their character, fiber. And the issue I set the most store by is whether they are honest with themselves. It's essential to be totally, brutally honest about how well—or how badly—things are going. It's also very difficult.

Too many businesspeople delude themselves. They want so much to believe that they listen only to what they want to hear and see only what they want to see. A good example is a top executive in the parallel-processing industry; he believed his engineering people when they told him the product would be ready on time, and he believed his marketing people when they told him how much they could sell. So he developed a sales staff and doubled the size of the plant and built up inventories before he had a product to sell. The computer was late because of some last-minute bugs, and he was stuck with it all. The first 98% of designing a computer is easy; the bugs always come up in the last 2%. Fixing the problems took time, which ate up all kinds of overhead. And when he was finally ready, he couldn't meet the company's forecasts—which had been unrealistic from the beginning.

This story illustrates well my thesis that strategy is easy, execution is hard. The company's product was two years ahead of its competition. Execution of the idea, however, was terrible. That the strategy was good is obvious now; several other manufacturers have entered the field and are doing very well. But the company has lost the competitive advantage it would have enjoyed if its management had been better.

I can cite a similar example, also from the computer industry. The three people who started the company were the president, the manager of the software division, and the manager of the hardware division. The two managers kept telling the president that things were going swimmingly, and he wanted to believe what they said. Then one day, faced with an order the company couldn't fill, the software division manager called the president, who was out of town, and let forth a blast that in essence said, "We've been making a lot of mistakes we haven't told you about. We're at least a year behind."

Now, that's a ridiculous situation; the president should have known the status of product development. He had enough background in the field, and he knew the managers well enough that he shouldn't have been caught by surprise. But he didn't look closely enough, and he didn't ask the right questions. In the meantime, the business had a rather large marketing and sales force. Then the question became whether to keep the sales force (which by this time was fully trained but doing nothing) or to let everyone go and wait for the software to be finished. If the latter, they'd have to hire and train a new sales force—a no-win situation either way.

Failure to be honest with yourself is a problem in any business, but it is especially disastrous in an entrepreneurial company, where the risk-reward stakes are so high. As an entrepreneur, you can't afford to make mistakes because you don't have the time and resources needed to recover. Big corporations can live with setbacks and delays in their "skunkworks"; in a start-up situation, you'd better be right the first time.

After being honest with yourself, the next most essential characteristic for the entrepreneur is to know whom to listen to and when to listen, and then which questions to ask. Sometimes CEOs listen only to what they want to hear because of fear of the truth; in other cases, it's because they are arrogant or have surrounded themselves with yes-men/women. A lot of managers simply will not accept criticism or suggestions from other people; they demand absolute loyalty from their subordinates and call disloyal anybody who tries to tell them something they don't want to hear.

It's usually easy to spot this trait by the way someone talks with outsiders about the organization. If an entrepreneur says, "This guy's lousy and that one doesn't know what she's doing, but I saved the company"— or if he or she explains how brilliantly he or she performed at his last job, in spite of being fired—I get wary. That kind of attitude is a red flag, like the statement, "I'll be honest with you": you know you're not getting the whole story.

To be sure, there's a thin line between refusing to accept criticism and sticking to your guns. Good entrepreneurs are committed to their ideas. In fact, I knew one company was in trouble when the CEO accepted almost everything I told him without argument or question. But some people have an almost perverse desire to prove to the world that their way is the right way—and the only way. I remember one CEO who had a great strategy—an idea for a unique computer architecture—but who refused to accept any advice on anything from anyone, including potential customers. He ended up with a product that had to be totally re-engineered and a weak staff. The company is now under new management and may be able to make something out of what is still a good idea, but the CEO's tunnel vision sure stalled it at the starting gate.

Another important quality—one that also has to do with taking a hard look at oneself and one's situation— is to know when to bring in skills from outside and what kind of skills.

As I see it, a company's growth has three stages. During the start-up, the entrepreneur does everything himself: he or she is involved in engineering the product, making sales calls, and so on. After a while, the company grows and others are hired to do these things—a vice president of sales, a vice president of engineering—but they report directly to him, and he or she still knows everything that's going on.

The company reaches the third stage when it hits, say $100 million to $200 million in sales. At that point, it's just too large for the president to be involved in all the doings. More management layers are in place and a fleet of executive vice presidents, and it now calls for entirely different skills to run the company than it did during its infancy. The president has to get work done by delegating it to other people and get information through two or more organizational layers.

The ideal would be a president who could manage a company at all three stages, starting the business from scratch and staying involved until retirement. Alfred Sloan at General Motors and Tom Watson at IBM were able to do just that, and the leaders of Teledyne and Intel have done it more recently.

But not all entrepreneurs can manage a large company. And many do not want to. Some people who relish business start-ups are simply not interested in running a formal, multi-tier organization. After Cray Computer grew to a fairly good size, for example, Seymour Cray wanted to get back to designing computers. Similarly, Apple Computer's Steve Wozniak and Steve Jobs (at least in the early stages) recognized that their genius was technical and promotional, not managerial, and that they needed experienced, professional managers to oversee their company's growth.

Other entrepreneurs have been less aware of their own limitations. Consider the experience of Diasonics and Daisy. Both flourished when they were small enough that their founders were able to control all aspects of the business. But they grew too fast, and the managers didn't realize that they now needed a different style of management and control. In both cases, a resounding initial success turned into an ignominious mess. As a result, both enterprises were reorganized.

Sometimes problems arise because the entrepreneur doesn't grasp the importance of strong management. I know of one young company that has already gone through two CEOs and is looking for a third. On the plus side, the men who founded the business acknowledged that they were engineers, not managers, and they went out and looked for a CEO. They considered their strategy so brilliant, though, that they figured anyone could carry if off. The first man they hired talked a good game but had been a disaster at two other corporations; eventually they had to let him go. He just couldn't manage the company. Then the directors hired another CEO who lasted only a few months. The company's product is still a good one, but without equally good leadership it may die in infancy.

The point of these examples is simple. If entrepreneurs do not have the skills required to manage the company, they should bring in an experienced professional. And they should never settle for someone mediocre by telling themselves that the business is such a winner that it doesn't need the management and controls that other companies do.

A great idea won't make it without great management. I am sometimes asked whether there is an "entrepreneurial personality." I suppose there are certain common qualities—a high energy level, strong commitment, and so on—but there are as many different personal styles as there are entrepreneurs. Henry Singleton of

Teledyne, for example, reminds me of Charles de Gaulle. He has a singleness of purpose, a tenacity that is just overpowering. He gives you absolute confidence in his ability to accomplish whatever he says he is going to do. Yet he's rather aloof, operating more or less by himself and dreaming up ideas in his corner office.

Max Palevsky, formerly at Scientific Data Systems (SDS), is, by contrast, a very warm person. At SDS he'd joke around with his employees and cajole them into doing what needed to be done. His very informal style was evidenced by his open shirt and feet up on the desk.

The CEO's personality is extremely important because it permeates the company, but there's no one style that seems to work better than another. What *is* important is to *have* a style. An "average Joe" won't inspire others and lead a business to success.

I look for an entrepreneur who can manage. A conventional manager isn't risk oriented enough to succeed with a new venture, while an entrepreneur without managerial savvy is just another promoter.

Good entrepreneurs are tough-minded, with themselves and with their teams. They can make hard decisions. They have to be able to say, "No, that won't work" to colleagues who come to them with ideas, or to say, "That's a good idea but we can't do it because we have other priorities." To make such professional judgments, managers should ideally be well versed in the technology on which the company is based.

There are exceptions, of course. John Sculley at Apple Computer comes immediately to mind. When Apple was looking for someone to fill the top slot, it instructed the executive recruiter to find a CEO with a technical computer background. But the recruiter asked Apple to consider someone from left field (from the soft-drink industry), and I need not point out that the results were excellent. It was a lucky fit. In fact, as far as the "secrets of entrepreneurial success" go, it's important to recognize that a little bit of luck helps and a lot of luck is even better.

Another company I know, formed by two young, inexperienced men, benefited from a lucky break. Though very knowledgeable, they seriously underestimated how long it would take to write the 1,500,000 lines of software code they needed to launch their product. Consequently, they were two years late in bringing the product to market. But the market was also slow in developing. If the product had been ready on time, the company probably would have gone bankrupt trying to sell something for which the market wasn't ready. As it turned out, the market and the product were ready at the same time, and the company could exploit the product without competition. Many business success stories are due at least in part to simple good luck.

I emphasize people rather than products, and for good reason. The biggest problem in starting high-tech businesses is the shortage of superior managers. There is too much money chasing too few good managers.

I have always preferred to wait and have entrepreneurs come to me, to approach me because they have a great desire to build a business. Now with all the megafunds available, it's often the venture capitalist who goes out to start a company and looks for people who can head it up.

Those who call us "vulture capitalists" do have a point; some venture capitalists lure away a company's best people, thus hampering its growth. How can an enterprise develop and thrive when its top executives are always being pursued to start new companies?

Unfortunately, in the high-tech industries, more and more businesses are being formed simply to make a buck. As for myself, though, I will continue to look for the best people, not the largest untapped market or the highest projected returns or the cleverest business strategy.

After all, a good idea, unless it's executed, remains only a good idea. Good managers, on the other hand, can't lose. If their strategy doesn't work, they can develop another one. If a competitor comes along, they can turn to something else. Great people make great companies, and that's the kind of company I want to be a part of.

**Originally published in November–December 1987**
**Reprint 87612**

# Bootstrap Finance

## *The Art of Start-ups*

AMAR BHIDE

## Executive Summary

ENTREPRENEURSHIP IS MORE POPULAR THAN EVER: courses are full, policymakers emphasize new ventures, managers yearn to go off on their own. Would-be founders often misplace their energies, however. Believing in a "big money" model of entrepreneurship, they spend a lot of time trying to attract investors instead of using wits and hustle to get their ideas off the ground.

A study of 100 of the 1989 *Inc.* "500" list of fastest growing U.S. start-ups attests to the value of bootstrapping. In fact, what it takes to start a business often conflicts with what venture capitalists require.

Investors prefer solid plans, well-defined markets, and track records. Entrepreneurs may be better off without them. Entrepreneurs are heavy on energy and enthusiasm but may be short on credentials. They thrive in rapidly changing environments where uncertain

149

prospects may scare off established companies. Rolling with the punches is often more important than formal plans. Striving to adhere to investors' criteria can diminish the flexibility—the try-it, fix-it aproach—an entrepreneur needs to make a new venture work.

Seven principles are basic for successful start-ups: get operational fast; look for quick break-even, cash-generating projects; offer high-value products or services that can sustain direct personal selling; don't try to hire the crack team; keep growth in check; focus on cash; and cultivate banks early.

Growth and change are the start-up's natural environment. But change is also the reward for success: just as ventures grow, their founders usually have to take a fresh look at everything again: roles, organization, even the very policies that got the business up and running.

---

ENTREPRENEURSHIP IS MORE CELEBRATED, studied, and desirable than ever. Business school students flock to courses on entrepreneurship. Managers, fearful of losing their step on the corporate ladder, yearn to step off on their own. Policymakers pin their hopes for job creation and economic growth on start-ups rather than on the once-preeminent corporate giants.

Belief in a "big money" model of entrepreneurship often accompanies this enthusiasm. Books and courses on new ventures emphasize fund raising: how to approach investors, negotiate deals, and design optimal capital structures. The media focuses on companies like Immulogic, which raised over $20 million in venture capital years before it expected to ship any products. Executives-turned-entrepreneurs try to raise millions from venture capitalists before they have sold a dime's worth of goods to customers. Lawmakers who favor entrepreneurship focus on tax incentives for venture capital and loan guarantees for start-ups.

This big-money model has little in common with the traditional low-budget start-up. Raising big money requires careful market research, well thought-out business plans, top-notch founding teams, sagacious boards, quarterly performance reviews, and devilishly complex financial structures. It is an environment in which analytical, buttoned-down professionals can make a seamless transition from the corporate world to the world of entrepreneurship. It is not the real world of the entrepreneur.

Without question, some start-ups powered by other people's money have rocketed to success. Mitch Kapor raised nearly $5 million of venture capital in 1982, enabling Lotus to launch 1–2–3 with the software industry's first serious advertising campaign. Significant initial capital is indeed a must in industries such as biotechnology or supercomputers where tens of millions of dollars have to be spent on R&D before any revenue is realized. But the fact is that the odds against raising big money are daunting. In 1987—a banner year—venture capitalists financed a grand total of 1,729 companies, of which 112 were seed financings and 232 were start-ups. In that same year, 631,000 new business incorporations were recorded.

Does this disparity mean that the United States needs more tax breaks, aggressive investors, and financially sophisticated entrepreneurs to channel venture capital to more start-up companies? Not at all. Over the past two years, my associates and I interviewed the founders of 100 companies on the 1989 *Inc.* "500" list of the fastest growing private companies in the United States. (See "The Study of Start-ups" on page 171.) The companies— Software 2000, Symplex Communications, Gammalink, and Modular Instruments, to mention just a few—are not household names. But they are the mainstay of the entrepreneurial revolution that politicians want to sustain and that so many people, managers and business students alike, hanker to join.

These interviews attest to the value of bootstrapping: launching ventures with modest personal funds. From this perspective, Ross Perot, who started EDS with $1,000 and turned it into a multibillion-dollar enterprise (and a presidential campaign), remains the rule, not the exception. More than 80% of these companies were financed through the founders' personal savings, credit cards, second mortgages, and in one case, "a $50 check that bounced." The median start-up capital was about $10,000. Furthermore, fewer than one-fifth of the bootstrappers had raised equity for follow-on financing in the five or more years that they had been in business. They relied on debt or retained earnings to grow.

What, then, is the problem? To quote Michael Lutz, CEO of Gammalink, a high-flying Silicon Valley venture that provides PC-to-facsimile communications services, "Raising money has become a disease. Entrepreneurs are wasting lots of brainpower scheming to raise money."

Professionals with MBAs and corporate experience are attempting to strike out on their own as never before: Michael Lutz, for example, is a physicist and Stanford MBA who worked at Hughes Aircraft and Raychem for 15 years before he joined up with a Silicon Valley guru to launch a new venture. Unlike the scrappy dropouts and malcontents of yore, however, these new entrepreneurs are unwilling to pursue business opportunities without raising big money first. Following text-book formulas for snaring investors, they attempt to recruit experienced teams. They write business plans with crisp executive summaries describing their propri-etary edge. If venture capitalists are unresponsive, they network with venture angels. Even today, they have heard there is more money than good ideas.

In fact, as Gammalink's founders learned, an entre-preneur's time is rarely well spent courting investors. De-spite a well-written business plan and excellent contacts, Lutz and his partner failed to attract venture capital in a year of trying. Eventually, they contributed $12,500 each to launch Gammalink. Years later, after their company was a proven success, it attracted $800,000 in unsolicited venture capital.

For the great majority of would-be founders, the biggest challenge is not raising money but having the wits and hustle to do without it. To that end, it helps to understand what it takes to start a business—and why that is likely to conflict with what venture capitalists require.

## A Poor Fit

Many an entrepreneur's hopes are dashed when a ven-ture capitalist rejects a promising business plan. But would-be founders should not interpret lack of interest from the investor community as a pronouncement that the business is doomed. Often entrepreneurs fail to qual-ify for venture capital not because their proposals are poor but because they do not meet the exacting criteria that venture capitalists must use.

Venture capitalists (and other investors in start-ups) are neither greedy nor shortsighted, as some disappointed entrepreneurs believe; they are simply inappropriate for most start-ups. Their criteria are understandably exacting: venture capitalists incur significant costs in investigating, negotiating, and monitoring investments. They can back only a few of the many entrepreneurs who seek funding, and they must anticipate that several investments will yield disappointing returns. One study of venture capital portfolios by Venture Economics, Inc. indicates that about 7% of the investments account for more than 60% of the profits, while a full one-third result in a partial or total loss. Each project must therefore represent a potential home run.

Start-ups, however, typically lack all or most of the criteria investors use to identify big winners: scale, proprietary advantages, well-defined plans, and well-regarded founders.

Most start-ups begin by pursuing niche markets that are too small to interest large competitors—or venture capitalists. Venture capitalists are hesitant to pursue small opportunities where even high-percentage returns will not cover their investment overhead. They favor products or services that address hundred-million-dollar markets. Legendary investor Arthur Rock goes so far as to limit his investments to businesses that have "the potential to change the world."

Few entrepreneurs start with a truly original concept or a plan to achieve a sustainable competitive advantage through a proprietary technology or brand name. Instead, they tend to follow "me too" strategies and, particularly in service businesses, to rely on superior execution and energy to generate profits. But it is hard for outside investors to evaluate an entrepreneur's ability to execute. Nor can they count on cashing in their investments in companies whose success cannot be sustained without the founders' capabilities.

Many entrepreneurs thrive in rapidly changing industries and niches where established companies are deterred by uncertain prospects. Their ability to roll with the punches is far more important than planning and foresight. Investors, on the other hand, prefer ventures with plausible, carefully thought-out plans to address well-defined markets. A solid plan reassures them about the competence of the entrepreneur and provides an objective yardstick for measuring progress and testing initial assumptions.

Finally, many entrepreneurs are long on energy and enthusiasm but short on credentials. Michael Dell was a freshman at the University of Texas when he started selling computer parts by mail order. Others are refugees from declining or oligopolistic industries, seeking new fields that offer more opportunity but where they lack personal experience.

Investors who see hundreds of business plans and entrepreneurs, however, cannot gauge or rely on the intangibles of personality. Thus Mitch Kapor was a good bet for investors because he already had a successful software product, Visiplot, under his belt before he launched Lotus. Bill Gates, on the other hand, a teenage college dropout when he launched Microsoft with his high school friend, Paul Allen, probably was not.

## The Hidden Costs of Other People's Money

Entrepreneurs who try to get investors to bend their criteria or create the perception that they meet those criteria do so at their peril. Several entrepreneurs pointed to the pitfalls of rushing to raise external financing.

Winning over investors too early, they said, can compromise your discipline and flexibility.

Bootstrapping in a start-up is like zero inventory in a just-in-time system: it reveals hidden problems and forces the company to solve them. "If we had had money," said Tom Davis of Modular Instruments, manufacturers of medical and research equipment, "we would have made more mistakes. This way, I wrote all the checks. I knew where the money was going."

There can also be problems with raising too much money. As one founder noted, "It is often easier to raise $5 million than $1 million because venture capitalists would rather not have to worry about a lot of tiny investments. But then you have $4 million you didn't need but spend anyhow."

George Brostoff, cofounder of Symplex Communications, which manufactures data communications equipment, agreed. "People in my industry think they need to be able to do x, y, and z at the outset. But the money gets burned up quickly, and it doesn't produce either profits or sales. Then they address the symptom—'we need more money'—instead of the underlying problems."

Diminished flexibility is often another consequence of premature funding. Start-ups entering new industries seldom get it right the first time. Success, especially in new and growing industries, follows many detours and unanticipated setbacks; strategies may have to be altered radically as events unfold. Failure to meet initial goals is a poor guide to future prospects. For example, Gammalink expected its first product, a high-speed modem, to be used to allow PCs to communicate with each other. Cofounder Lutz thought he had done his homework and was sure there was a market for the product. But, in fact, buyers never materialized. Gammalink next tried to sell its modem in volume to Dialog as part of a new database Dialog was developing for corporate attorneys. But the database never got off the ground, and Dialog bought a mere three modems.

Lutz and his partner had to rethink their strategy again. This time they targeted large companies with dispersed PCs. They sent out 5,000 mailers at $1 each and got only 25 responses. Twenty-four of them led nowhere but the twenty-fifth, from BMW of North America, said, "This is the product we've been waiting for." BMW bought a few, then placed a blanket order for $700,000."

Outside investors, however, can hinder entrepreneurs from following the try-it, fix-it approach required in the uncertain environments in which start-ups flourish. The prospect of a radical change in course presents outside investors with a quandary: "Was the original concept wrong or was it poorly executed?" The entrepreneur is sure the new strategy will work but was just as confident about the original plan. The investors wonder, "Are we being fooled twice?" Supporting the proposed new strategy rather than, say, changing management is an act of faith that requires investors to discard what seems like hard evidence of poor planning, bad judgment, or overselling.

For their part, entrepreneurs may develop the confidence to push back against investors once the business has taken shape. But in the early years, they tend to avoid direct challenges. Instead, they stick with their original plans even when they begin to lose faith in them because they fear that radical shifts will draw the wrong kind of scrutiny. The former CEO of an advanced materials company described the pressure to stick with untenable strategies that outside investors can create.

"When we started, well-defined markets for our materials did not exist. My first job as CEO was to figure out what product market we would go after, so I hit the road for about three months. I identified a product—aluminum oxide substrates—but by the time we got to market, the competition had improved and our substrates never really took off. I realized that, given our size, we should have been manufacturing to order rather than for the market at large. But by that time, we were already stumbling and I was losing credibility with the investors. They weren't interested in a new strategy. They just wanted the substrates to be profitable. I wish I had stood my ground and said, 'I'm turning off the furnace tomorrow.' But I didn't quite have the guts to do that."

Conflicts between investors in a business and its day-to-day managers are a fact of life. They are less debilitating, however, after the entrepreneur has the credibility to be a true partner. Entrepreneurs who are unsure of their markets or who don't have the experience to deal with investor pressure are better off without other people's capital, even if they can somehow get investors to overlook sketchy plans and limited credentials.

## Flying on Empty

Starting a business with limited funds requires a different strategy and approach than launching a well-capitalized venture. Compaq Computer, for example, was a venture capitalist's dream. Rod Canion, Jim Harris, and Bill Murto had all been senior managers at Texas Instruments, and they had a well-formulated plan to take on IBM with a technologically superior product. Seasoned investor Ben Rosen helped Canion raise $20 million in start-up capital—funds that allowed the new business to behave like a big company from the start. Canion could attract experienced managers by offering them generous salaries and participation in a stock option plan. Compaq also had a national dealer network established within a year of exhibiting its first prototype. Sales totaled more than $100 million in the first year.

Bootstrappers need a different mind-set and approach. Principles and practices imported from the corporate world will not serve them as well as the following axioms drawn from successful entrepreneurs.

**1. Get operational quickly.** Bootstrappers don't mind starting with a copycat idea targeted to a small market. Often that approach works well. Imitation saves the costs of market research, and the start-up entering a small market is unlikely to face competition from large, established companies.

Of course, entrepreneurs do not reap fame and fortune if their enterprises remain marginal. But once they are in the flow of business, opportunities often turn up that they would not have seen had they waited for the big idea.

Consider, for example, the evolution of Eaglebrook Plastics, now one of the largest high-density polyethylene recyclers in the United States. Eaglebrook was founded in 1983 by Andrew Stephens and Bob Thompson, who had been chemical engineering students at Purdue. At first, they bought plastic scrap, had it ground by someone else, then sold it, primarily to the pipe industry. One year later, they bought a used $700 grinder, which they operated at night so that they could sell during the day. Soon they moved up to a $25,000 grinder, but they only began to hire when they couldn't keep up with demand.

In 1985, the company developed an innovative process for purifying paper-contaminated plastic scrap— and began to make a name for itself in the industry. In

1987, with the profitability of scrap declining, the partners turned to recycling plastic bottles, a novel idea at
the time. Next came plastic lumber made from recycled
materials and then, most recently, a joint venture with
the National Polyethylene Recycling Corporations to
manage their styrofoam recycling operations. Few if any
of these opportunities could have been foreseen at the
outset.

**2. Look for quick break-even, cash-generating pro-
jects.** The rule in large companies and well-funded
enterprises is to stick to the basic strategy. Not so with
the bootstrapped start-up. Profit opportunities that
might be regarded as distractions in a large company are
immensely valuable to the entrepreneur. A business that
is making money, elegantly or not, builds credibility in
the eyes of suppliers, customers, and employees, as well
as self-confidence in the entrepreneur.

For example, Raju Patel launched NAC with the
ambitious goal of serving the Baby Bells created by the
AT&T breakup. NAC's first offering, however, was a low-
end auto-dialer targeted to the many start-ups that were
reselling long-distance services from carriers like MCI.
"We thought it would be appropriate to get a cash gen-
erator to make us known as a new entrant," Patel
explained. Then at a conference, Patel happened to meet
a reseller who mentioned his need for more accurate
customer-billing capability. NAC stopped work on the
auto-dialer and rapidly developed and shipped a billing
system. The system was later phased out as the customers themselves began to fold. But its quick, albeit
short-lived, success helped NAC attract the engineers it
needed to grow because it enabled Patel to offer security
as well as the excitement of a start-up. "We weren't seen

as a revolving-door company. We were able to offer health plans and other benefits comparable to those of large companies." More ambitious products, aimed at the Bell companies, followed. Today NAC is well established as a small systems supplier to the Bell companies.

Robert Grosshandler's Softa group also used the cash flow from one business to develop another. "Our property management software was funded by selling hardware and peripherals to *Fortune* '500' companies. It was low-margin, but it had fast turnaround. Goods arrived in the morning and left in the evening. Our software, on the other hand, took nearly a year to develop."

Many entrepreneurs sustained themselves by part-time consulting. In the early days, says Robert Pemberton of Software 2000, which develops and distributes business applications software, consulting accounted for more than 50% of the revenue of the business.

**3. Offer high-value products or services that can sustain direct personal selling.** Getting a customer to give up a familiar product or service for that of a shaky start-up is arguably the most important challenge an entrepreneur faces. "When we first started selling," Modular's Davis recalled, "people would ask, 'When are you going to go out of business?'"

Many entrepreneurs underestimate the marketing costs entailed in overcoming customer inertia and conservatism, especially with respect to low-value or impulse goods. Launching a new packaged food product without substantial financial resources, for example, is an oft-undertaken and futile endeavor. Creating a serious business means persuading hundreds of thousands of customers to try out a new $5 mustard or jam in place of their usual brand. Without millions of dollars of mar-

ket research, advertising, and promotion, this can be a
hopeless task.

Therefore, successful entrepreneurs often pick high-
ticket products and services where their personal passion, salesmanship, and willingness to go the extra mile
can substitute for a big marketing budget. As John
Mineck, cofounder of Practice Management Systems,
said, "People buy a salesperson. They bought me and I
had no sales experience. But I truly believed our systems
and software for automating doctors' offices would
work—so the customers did too. Also, we did an awful
lot for our first clients; if they wanted something, we'd
deliver. We were providing service and support long
before that became a cliché."

Like Mineck, three-quarters of the founders we interviewed were also their company's chief or only salesperson. They sold directly, usually to other businesses. Only
10% used brokers or distributors, and only 14% offered
consumer goods or services. The median unit sale was
$5,000, an amount high enough to support direct per-
sonal selling and also, presumably, to get the attention
of buyers. The few consumer items we encountered were
also important purchases for buyers: a $20,000 recre-
ational vehicle from Chariot Eagle or an SAT preparation course from the *Princeton Review,* rather than a $5
to $10 staple that consumers purchase without great
thought.

Overcoming customer inertia is easier and cheaper if
a product offers some tangible advantage over substitutes. Our successful entrepreneurs overcame reserva-
tions about their long-term viability by selling concrete
performance characteristics—faster chips and fourth-
generation language software, for instance—rather than
intangible attributes like a tangier sauce or more evoca-

tive perfume. "We had no track record and no commercial office—I was running the company from my home," recalled Prabhu Goel, founder of Gateway Design Automation, which supplies CAE software tools. "So we went after the most sophisticated users who had a problem that needed to be solved. The risk of dealing with us was small compared with the risk of not solving the problem."

Concrete product attributes also contribute to important serendipitous sales. With just a prototype, Brostoff of Symplex got an order for 100 units from Mead Data, his first significant customer. "We didn't call them, they called us," Brostoff told us. "A high-level manager read an article about us that suggested our product could offer customers like Mead dramatic cost savings—as much as $55,000 annually on a one-time investment of $10,000 to $20,000. Mead had an on-line database product and was looking to cut costs."

Intangibles like responsiveness and attention do provide greater leverage for entrepreneurial selling in service and distribution businesses. Clay Teramo, founder of Computer Media Technology, a computer supplies distributor, described the way he used service—and the customer's perception of service—to make up for the fact that early on his competitors had far more resources. When someone called with a next-day order that Computer Media couldn't handle, Teramo would tell them that he didn't have the whole order in stock and ask if he could fill part of it the next day and part later on. If the customer agreed, he'd follow up personally to make sure everything had gone smoothly and to say thanks. As Teramo pointed out, his competitors could probably have filled the whole order at once. But the customer wouldn't think he had received any special service.

Carol Russell of Russell Personnel Services took a similar approach. "Our business is done on the cult of personality," she said. "You roll up your sleeves and say to the customer, 'Hi, I'm Carol Russell, and I'm going to work overtime to get you employed or employees.' In a people business, being a young company and visible is an advantage. In the large services, you won't meet the Mr. Olstens or the Mr. Kellys."

**4. Forget about the crack team.** It is not unusual for investor-backed start-ups to hire CFOs or marketing managers at $100,000 a year. Bootstrappers cannot afford this investment. Besides, if the entrepreneurs' credentials aren't strong enough to attract investors, they are even less likely to be able to attract a highly qualified team. Novices who are urged to recruit a well-rounded team rarely succeed. Steve Jobs had his pick of talent for NeXT; Apple, however, was built by youthful exuberance.

The start-ups that we studied attracted employees by providing them with opportunities to upgrade skills and build résumés, rather than by offering cash or options. Their challenge was to find and motivate diamonds in the rough.

"I never hired experienced people," said Bohdan Associates's founder Peter Zacharkiw, "and there are very few college graduates here. My vice president of sales was the best curb painter around—but that's the secret. He'll always be the best at what he does. Personality and common sense are the most important things that people here have."

John Greenwood's first employee at Micron Separations was a 62-year-old machine shop worker who had just been laid off. His production manager was a

Worcester Polytechnic Institute graduate who had been working as an accountant in a company he hated and was looking for another job. "We never attempted to lure anybody away from another company," Greenwood told us. "One, we were cheap. Two, we had moral reasons—if we went under and it didn't work out for them, we wouldn't feel so bad. We never felt that we had an inadequate pool, though. I believe the people in the 'unemployment market' are just as good if not better than the people in the employment market. And we have no prejudice against people who've been fired. My partner and I started Micron after we were fired! In large companies, people tend to get fired for lack of political skills."

Not all entrepreneurs were so fortunate, however. Some had to cope with employees who had neither the formal qualifications nor the right temperament and attitude for their jobs. "Large companies can hire by credentials and screen people carefully," said Robert Rodriguez of National Communications Sales Promotion, a Miami-based company that helps customers manage their sales promotion campaigns. "We needed to have things happen quickly and took people on the basis of their initial presentation. But many didn't do what they said they could."

**5. Keep growth in check.** Start-ups that failed because they could not fund their growth are legion. Successful bootstrappers take special care to expand only at the rate they can afford and control. For example, they tend to invest in people or capacity only when there is no alternative, not in advance of needs. "Our first product was done before the company was founded," said Warren Anderson, founder of Anderson

Soft-Teach. "I produced it, paid for it, took it to a trade show, and we started taking orders before we hired people. It was like brick-laying. We added one layer at a time. We didn't have a venture capitalist putting up money for us—just $30,000 of our own money—and we were selling our tapes for $200 each."

Keeping growth in check is not only financially prudent but it also helps the entrepreneur develop management skills and iron out problems under less pressure. Even entrepreneurs who don't have to make radical changes in strategy may have to make adjustments as they learn about the nuances of their chosen industry. Learning the nuts and bolts of running a business is particularly important for first-time entrepreneurs. Stephanie DiMarco and her partner encountered few major surprises when they started Advent Software. Nevertheless, in the early years, DiMarco noted, they felt constrained by their lack of knowledge and held back on their growth. "Instead of trying to create an organization, I wanted to prove myself first. It was important for me to learn the business before I hired someone else. I had never managed anyone before." After the partners learned how to run a business, Advent enjoyed explosive growth.

In their rush to grow, some entrepreneurs told us, they took on customers who nearly put them under. "When you are new and cold-calling customers," observed Fred Zak of Venture Graphics, "the business that comes your way is usually from customers who can't pay their bills or shop only on price—the worst kind of customer base. About 40% of our early work came from deadbeats. I soon determined that I would have to call on them personally, and I'd show up unannounced. It was nerve-racking, but they would pay us off so that they wouldn't have to see me again!"

Some will argue that controlled growth and reactive investments allow competitors to preempt the market. In fact, there are few businesses that entrepreneurs can realistically expect to start in which grabbing dominant market share first is crucial. In mature service industries such as temporary services, advertising, or public relations (where many of our entrepreneurs found their niches), dominance, early or late, is out of the question. But even in high-tech fields, first-mover advantages are often short-lived. Compaq's early start in the IBM clone market did not thwart later bootstrapped entrants like Dell Computer and AST Research. Similarly, Word-Perfect, today's dominant player in word processing software, was not among the first half-dozen entrants.

Frequent changes in technology allow entrepreneurs who miss one wave while getting organized to ride the next. Several computer distributors we interviewed missed getting in on the first generation of PCs and so could not obtain the all-important "IBM Authorized Dealer" medallion. But the growth of Novell and local area networks created new opportunities, which the established, first-generation competitors, engrossed in traditional products, couldn't easily take advantage of.

**6. Focus on cash, not on profits, market share, or anything else.**  A well-funded start-up can afford to pursue several strategic goals; bootstrappers usually cannot. For example, cash-constrained start-ups cannot "buy business." In venture capital-backed or intrapreneurial ventures, it may be feasible for a start-up to sell at a loss in anticipation of scale economies or learning curve advantages. But the bootstrapper must earn healthy margins, practically from day one, not only to cover the company's costs but also to finance growth. "I learned early that it is better to have a low-profile, positive cash-flow job than a high-ego, negative cash-flow job," said Keith Kakacek, founder of the commercial insurance group, SIR Lloyds. "If the market doesn't pay for your business—and you can't develop positive cash flow—you probably don't have a good enough concept."

Getting terms from suppliers and timely payments from customers are critical in managing cash. Ron Norris of Automotive Caliper Exchange told us he started with and maintained positive cash flow from operations in spite of rapid growth. Building on contacts developed over 20 years, he went to six suppliers and asked for 90- to 120-day terms for one time only on his first order. All but one agreed. Now established, Norris gives modest discounts to customers who pay quickly. But he won't tolerate any "gray" whatever. If a customer doesn't pay in 30 days—and hasn't called to explain why—the company won't sell to him any longer.

Equally important is knowing when to spend and when to economize. Successful bootstrappers are generally cheap, except in one or two crucial areas. "We began in a modest room," recalled Brian Cornish of Oscor Medical Corporation, which makes instruments for microsurgery. "We licked stamps instead of buying a Pitney Bowes machine. We never had plush offices or any of the other trappings of some start-ups. But we made sure we got the very best microscopes."

**7. Cultivate banks before the business becomes creditworthy.** It is common wisdom that bank loans can be a cheap alternative to external equity and crucial for financing additional inventory or larger receivables. But bank financing is often unavailable for start-ups, as many entrepreneurs we interviewed discovered.

Winning bankers over requires preparation and careful timing.

Consider, for example, how Phil Bookman of Silton-Bookman went about managing his company's bank relationship. Bookman did not even try to borrow until his software company was creditworthy. But he made sure that the company kept good books, that its records were immaculate, and that its balance sheets were sound. In addition, he opened accounts with a big bank's local branch and from time to time asked the branch manager's advice to familiarize him with Silton-Book-man's business. Then when the company had been in business for the requisite three years, Bookman went to the banker with the company's business plan. "He looked over the numbers," Bookman explained, "and said, 'It looks like you need a $50,000 term loan.' We knew that all along, but it was important that he suggested it. We got the loan and paid it back, then used the same method the next year to get a line of credit."

## Abandoning the Rules

Growth and change create difficult transitions for all entrepreneurial companies. The challenges faced by a charismatic founder in letting go and designing an organization in which authority and responsibility are appropriately distributed are well-known. The bootstrapper's problem is particularly acute, however. To build a durable business—as opposed to a personal project or an alternative to employment—successful entrepreneurs not only have to modify their personal roles and organization, but they may also have to effect a U-turn and abandon the very policies that allowed them to get up and running with limited capital. As part of these changes, the start-up may have to:

- Emerge from its niche and compete with a large company. When *Princeton Review* was launched, it competed with private tutors of uneven quality in Manhattan. To become a nationally franchised operation, the company had to confront the well-established Stanley Kaplan chain.

- Offer more standard, less customized products. "We did a lot of things for our first clients that we wouldn't do today," said Practice Management Systems's Mineck. "The easiest thing for a salesperson to say is, 'we can do it,' and the hardest thing is, 'we can't do this for you.'"

- Bring critical services in-house. Automotive Caliper never hired an in-house controller because it didn't need the expertise. But it does have its own fleet of trucks. The smartly dressed drivers project the company's image, and they provide an important source of information because they can find out things the sales force cannot see.

- Change management's focus from cash flow to strategic goals. Phil Bookman, a self-confessed "cash management fanatic" in the early years, pointed out how important—and hard—it was to shift gears later on and remind people that they had to think more about the big picture and worry less about the little expenditures.

- Recruit higher priced talent, perhaps encouraging early employees to move on. Sometimes the need to turn over early employees and hire professionals in their place is an obvious business decision. At National Communications Sales Promotion, for example, all but two of Rodriguez's original employees left within a few years. A few had simply grown stale, but most were fired for unprofessional behavior or because their attitude was bad. To get people with the right attitude and experience, Rodriguez began to pay more and to look for different qualities: MBAs with family responsibilities replaced "swinging singles" who weren't above making side deals.

More often, however, replacing the start-up's early team presents the entrepreneur with one of the most difficult transitions he or she must confront. At Rizzo Associates, an engineering and environmental services company, four of the first seven employees had to leave because they could not grow with the company. "We promised employees substantial opportunities in terms of personal growth and sold them a future," William Rizzo recalled. "But we did not tell them that they had to live up to that future. In time, we had to bring people in over them, and they felt their future was sealed off. Eventually they said, 'The hell with you.' Today I would be more candid about the fact that our promises are contingent on their performance."

Changes in strategy or personnel at more "professionally" designed and launched start-ups may be less dramatic or personally wrenching. But hard as making these changes may be, they are unavoidable for the entrepreneur who succeeds enough to turn a start-up venture into an ongoing business.

---

## The Study of Start-ups

LESSONS ABOUT ENTREPRENEURSHIP are often drawn from individual case studies, which provide rich but potentially idiosyncratic data, or from survey statistics that reveal little of the hows and whys of success. In pursuit of both depth and breadth, I recently completed a far-reaching field study of start-ups. With the help of Research Associates Kevin Hinton and Laura Pochop and Professor Howard Stevenson, I interviewed 100 company founders about how they overcame the daunting obstacles that confront start-ups.

The companies in the study came from the 1989 *Inc.* "500" list, a compilation of the fastest growing privately held companies in the United States that had sales of at least $100,000 in 1983. (The average company on this list had 1988 revenues of about $15 million, 135 employees, and a five-year sales growth record of 1,407%.) I narrowed my list of prospective interviewees to companies founded after 1982, on the grounds that the start-up history of older companies would be more difficult to obtain.

Finding a representative cross section of start-ups was a challenge. Since many incorporations are just attempts at self-employment or poorly conceived ventures that would say little about starting new businesses, I could not simply draw from the hundreds of thousands of new businesses incorporated every year. At the same time, I also wanted to avoid the few billion-dollar successes like Federal Express or Microsoft, which the typical entrepreneur cannot realistically hope to emulate. My sample provided a happy middle ground. The *Inc.* list's requirement of a five-year track record of rapid growth helped eliminate low-potential or "born to fail" ventures. And with 500 companies on the list, I avoided "outliers" that succeeded because of the unusual talent (or luck) of the founder.

To get the start-ups' stories in all their complexity, I chose to conduct face-to-face interviews rather than send out a mail survey. Start-ups are characterized by close relationships among financing, marketing strategies, hiring, and control systems that would be hard to capture through a structured survey. Since executives of successful companies are inundated with mail surveys, response rates are generally low. Although we had some difficulty in contacting entrepreneurs and scheduling appointments, only a few declined to be interviewed.

Each interview lasted from one to three hours. Usually two researchers took handwritten notes, which were then compiled into a single transcript and returned to the interviewees for review.

To my knowledge, this is one of the broadest, most in-depth studies of U.S. start-ups. Where other field studies have focused on limited geographic regions or industries, we visited over 20 cities and towns in a dozen states to interview entrepreneurs in a wide range of businesses. Researchers who have tackled similarly broad samples have relied on mail surveys.

Reflecting *Inc.*'s criteria, my sample was biased toward very high-growth companies. But the skew actually reinforces my findings about the importance of bootstrapping: start-ups that grow more slowly are even less likely to need or be able to attract outside risk capital.

**Originally published in November–December 1992**
**Reprint 92601**

# Commercializing Technology

## *What the Best Companies Do*

T. MICHAEL NEVENS,

GREGORY L. SUMME, AND

BRO UTTAL

## Executive Summary

SOME COMPANIES ARE FAR BETTER AT COMMERCIAL-
IZING TECHNOLOGY than their similarly sized rivals.
They bring twice as many new products, incorporating
twice as many technologies, to twice as many markets in
half the time.

The ability to commercialize technology is for many
businesses a matter of survival. It is linked to competitive
leadership in a variety of markets, like copiers, computers, automobiles, and pharmaceuticals. In the mid-
1980s, when Minolta eclipsed Canon as the leader in
35mm cameras, Canon focused on strengthening its
commercialization skills. Determined to win with superior
optical and electronic technology and to cut the development period in half, it built a sophisticated lens-grinding plant and central lab and encouraged divisional

managers to be accessible to project managers. In 1986, Canon's camera division introduced two products that exploited a breakthrough in lens technology and regained the lead by the end of that year.

Companies that want to improve their commercialization capability can learn a lot from organizations that are good at it. Leaders like Canon, Xerox, and Hewlett-Packard describe their approaches to commercialization in strikingly similar terms. They treat commercialization as a system and apply to it the same discipline they use in manufacturing. They make it a priority, state it in terms of measurable goals, build cross-functional skills, and encourage aggressive action.

---

Just as quality and manufacturing excellence were key to competitiveness in the 1980s, superior commercialization of technology will be crucial in the 1990s. In the coming decade, businesses will rise and fall depending on whether they discipline their commercialization efforts. Some companies—like Canon, Philips, and Merck—already have the capability to bring sophisticated technology-based products to market faster and more often than competitors that treat commercialization as a purely intuitive, creative process. Most other companies will be compelled to develop this capability if are to thrive.

Over the past year, we have examined the difference between leaders and laggards in commercialization in the United States, Japan, and Europe. (See "About the Study" on page 199.) Our study found that leading companies. . .

- commercialize two to three times the number of new products and processes as do their competitors of comparable size.

- incorporate two to three times as many technologies in their products.

- bring their products to market in less than half the time and

- compete in twice as many product and geographic markets.

These differences are not one-time occurrences that reflect specific product introductions, nor are they limited to certain nations. The study found that the critical differences between high-performing companies and low-performing companies. . .

- were sustained over multiyear periods and

- were as great in Japan as in America or Europe.

As part of the study, managers were asked to describe their commercialization processes. An interesting pattern emerged. Companies that are good at commercialization did not describe processes that are idiosyncratic to their organizations. Rather. . .

- high performers explained their success in strikingly similar terms and

- low performers did not describe their businesses in the terms high performers used.

In short, the study found large differences among companies' abilities to commercialize technology, and the good companies seemed to be doing certain things that the poor companies were not. While many businesses treat the commercialization process as a series of separate steps or an inherently creative task that should not be tightly managed, the good companies view commercialization as a highly disciplined system. They apply to the total commercialization process the basic principles for improving manufacturing quality: they establish it as a top priority, set measurable goals for ongoing improvement, develop the necessary organizational skills, and encourage managers to take aggressive action. They see it as management's job to ensure that handoffs and communication are rapid and smooth, and they pay relentless attention to improving the process. (See "The Commercialization Process," on page 200 for more about this).

Further, the study found a strong linkage between an organization's competitiveness and its ability to commercialize technology. In many markets—such as copiers, facsimile machines, computers, automobiles, semiconductor production equipment, and pharmaceuticals—industry leadership clearly depends on superior commercialization skill. In these and a growing number of industries, companies that are first to market with products based on advanced technologies command higher margins and gain share. Companies that spin out variants more rapidly and leverage their core technologies across more markets earn higher returns. Superior commercialization skill is, then, among the most important competitive challenges managers will face in the coming decade.

## The Commercialization Imperative

The ability to commercialize technology, to move a product from concept to market quickly and efficiently, is crucial in light of changes in the business environment. First among these now-familiar trends is the increasing proliferation of new technologies and the speed with which they render previous technologies obsolete. Empirical evidence of this trend is abundant and includes the shrinking life cycles of many products.

Typewriters are one example. The first modern generation of typewriters was mechanical and dominated the market for some 25 years, but subsequent generations of typewriters have had progressively short lives: 15, 7, and 5 years. That is, it took 25 years for sales of mechanical typewriters to fall below sales of electromechanical ones; 15 years for electromechanical models to give way to entirely electric ones; 7 years for sales of electric models to be over-taken by sales of microprocessor-controlled machines; and 5 years for sales of first-generation, microprocessor-controlled models to be exceeded by sales of second-generation machines.

Injectable cephalosporins—drugs that are prescribed for various bacterial infections—followed the same pattern in the West German hospital market. The first generation of these drugs was introduced there in 1965. Not until 1977 did sales of second generation cephalosporins surpass those of the original products. But a fourth generation began to overtake the third in only one year.

Technological innovations also are spreading very rapidly, a result in part of the growth of research consortia and international suppliers. Indeed, it is difficult to point to an important technology breakthrough in recent years that was—and remained—truly proprietary.

And technology is increasingly expensive. Perhaps the most powerful and familiar example of the rapid cost inflation of developing base technologies is the silicon process technology used in DRAM production. The process

technology for a 256K DRAM, which was state-of-the-art
in 1985, cost about $100 million to develop and required a
$100 million capital investment in the production facil-
ity. The next generation of DRAMs had a 1Mb capacity,
cost about $250 million, and required a $200 million capital investment. The generation after that, 4Mb DRAMs,
will end up costing close to $500 million and requiring a
manufacturing investment of nearly half a billion dollars.

Another factor driving the increased importance of
commercialization capability is the fragmentation of
markets—the result of higher real per capita incomes
and more sophisticated consumers. In the U.S. automobile market, for instance, the number of segments rose
by one-third in seven years—from 18 in 1978 to 24 in
1985. (See the exhibit "The Number of Market Segments
Is Increasing.") Many of these market segments remain
untapped until a company introduces a product offering
that is tailored to that niche.

These competitive realities make the capability to
commercialize technology at least as important as traditional sources of advantage such as scale, skilled labor,
possession of proprietary technology, and access to capital. Companies that possess the capability to bring technology to the market can often drive out competitors.
Companies that lack it may see even prominent market
positions quickly erode. Xerox and certain Japanese
microcomputer printer manufacturers learned this lesson the hard way.

Xerox dominated the copier market for many years,
but in the mid-1970s, its four- to seven-year development cycle cost it that lead. In 1976, competitors like
Canon began introducing mid-range plain-paper copiers
in quick succession. Between 1976 and 1982, more than
90 new models reached the market, most of them mid-

range machines, and Xerox's 82% share of the total market fell by half. Since Xerox had no competitive mid-range model of its own, it embarked on a crash program to develop one. But the company's commercialization process faltered under extreme pressure. The resulting product—the 3300 model—was unreliable and too expensive. Moreover, Xerox was unable to introduce

## The Number of Market Segments Is Increasing

**Segments of the U.S. Automobile Market**

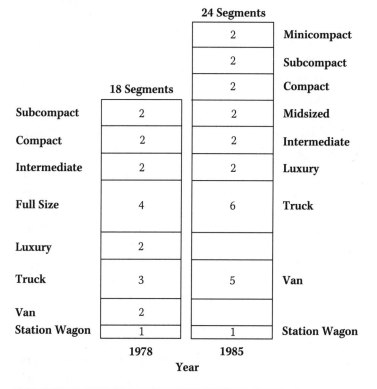

| | 1978 (18 Segments) | | 1985 (24 Segments) | |
|---|---|---|---|---|
| | | | 2 | Minicompact |
| | | | 2 | Subcompact |
| | | | 2 | Compact |
| Subcompact | 2 | | 2 | Midsized |
| Compact | 2 | | 2 | Intermediate |
| Intermediate | 2 | | 2 | Luxury |
| Full Size | 4 | | 6 | Truck |
| Luxury | 2 | | | |
| Truck | 3 | | 5 | Van |
| Van | 2 | | | |
| Station Wagon | 1 | | 1 | Station Wagon |

**Year**

Source: *World's Automotive Yearbooks*

variants quickly enough to position the 3300 as part of a product family covering several segments of the mid-market.

Canon, on the other hand, had developed great skill at commercializing technology. It produced a number of technology innovations and launched four low-end and mid-range copiers in quick succession with speeds, respectively, of 12, 20, 30, and 40 copies per minute. It gained a solid position in the mid-range market, mostly at Xerox's expense.

Xerox has since strengthened its commercialization skills. During its turnaround in the early 1980s, the company cut development cycles from seven to as little as two years, and it introduced more than six major technical innovations in the five models that comprise its "10 series." It achieved a three-year lead over competitors in these technologies and began to reverse its decline in market share.

Just as Xerox dominated the copier market in the early 1970s, Japanese companies practically owned the microcomputer-printer business in the early 1980s. But in the mid-1980s, Hewlett-Packard used its ability to commercialize technology to take share away from the entrenched players. In quick succession, H-P introduced a broad line of printers based on innovative laser, ink-jet, and software technologies. Over the past six years, it has seized a significant share of the market, including nearly 60% of the U.S. market for desktop laser printers.

## Measuring Commercialization Capability

Companies like Hewlett-Packard that have the capability to manage the commercialization process differ from other organizations in four respects. They get products or processes to market faster, use those technologies in products across a wider range of markets, introduce more products, and incorporate a greater breadth of technologies in them. Thus time to market, range of markets, number of products, and breadth of technologies are good measures of a company's ability to commercialize—and to compete.

## TIME TO MARKET

When base technologies are widely available and product life cycles are short, getting to market quickly is essential. For one thing, the company that is first to market often can command premium pricing because of its de facto monopoly. In the European market for car radios, for example, the first to market typically can charge 20% more than a competitor that introduces a comparable product a year later.

Those early premiums are important since prices decline rapidly as soon as competition arrives. Companies typically try to offset the price declines by improving production efficiency, but the resulting savings are not necessarily enough to compensate for sliding prices and to recover high development costs.

Early entrants also achieve volume break points in purchasing and production sooner than laggards, and they gain market share. In some industries, like prescription pharmaceuticals, the market-share rewards for being first are especially great. In that industry, the regulatory process imposes irreducible delays, and physicians' prescribing habits tend to be slow to change, which makes it difficult for later entrants to catch up.

Many managers fail to acknowledge the benefits of getting to the market first. The same program managers who know to the penny what an additional engineer will cost and what profits will be lost if the company misses manufacturing cost targets seldom can quantify the losses associated with a six-month slip in the development process. They willingly slow down the development process to contain the project budget or to hit their cost targets. What they don't know is the overall economics: assuming that the market grows 20% a year, that prices drop 12% a year, and that the product life cycle is five years, launching a laser printer six months behind schedule can reduce the product's cumulative profits by one-third. In contrast, under the same set of assumptions, a development cost overrun of 30% will trim cumulative profits by only 2.3%. (See the exhibit "How Problems Developing a Printer Affect Profits.")

## How Problems Developing a Printer Affect Profits

**Percentage decrease in cumulative profit**

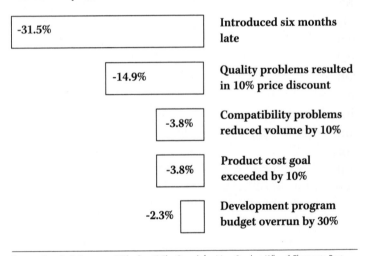

| | |
|---|---|
| -31.5% | Introduced six months late |
| -14.9% | Quality problems resulted in 10% price discount |
| -3.8% | Compatibility problems reduced volume by 10% |
| -3.8% | Product cost goal exceeded by 10% |
| -2.3% | Development program budget overrun by 30% |

Source: *Don G. Reineertsen, "Whodunnit? The Search for New Product Killers," Electronic Business,* July 1983, pp. 62–66.

## RANGE OF MARKETS

The cost of developing technologies is high—and rising. Companies that incur these costs must spread them across as many product and geographic markets as possible. Otherwise, they will be unable to recover costs, maintain price parity, and renew development efforts— all of which are essential to competitiveness. For example, the telecommunications industry spent a total of $1.2 billion on R&D for telephone switches in 1983 and $1.9 billion in 1988. That represents a 10% compound yearly increase over the five-year period. The increases reflect existing companies' attempts to add new features to their software systems—not new entrants to the market. At the same time, prices for central-office switches declined about 8% a year. Obviously, there was intense pressure to find ways to recover that spending.

One way to spread costs is to leverage core technologies across multiple product and geographic markets. In the late 1970s, Northern Telecom anticipated that developing the software for its digital switch was going to be expensive, so it made an aggressive drive to spread the technology across many markets at the same time. To compensate for limited marketing resources, it formed international alliances with partners that could tailor the switch to national markets where Northern Telecom's own distribution networks were relatively weak. Northern Telecom also used part of the software in several product areas like PBXs, hybrid analog-digital switches, and fully configured central-office switches.

Honda, too, spreads the costs of innovation over several product markets. When it invested heavily to develop multivalve cylinder heads with self-adjusting valves, for example, it applied the technology to motorcycles, cars, lawn mowers, and power-generation equipment. Similarly, Canon exploits its basic investments in optics and lens grinding across the markets for photolithography, cameras, and copiers. It has used the miniaturized motors from its photolithography equipment in its cameras and is now incorporating them in copiers. Hewlett-Packard uses technology from its instrumentation business in half a dozen highly differentiated markets, from oscilloscopes to cardiac analyzers.

Joint ventures, technology crosslicensing, and marketing relationships are effective solutions for companies that lack the ability to spread technology costs. International marketing alliances have worked well for drug companies.

## NUMBER OF PRODUCTS

Market fragmentation creates opportunities for companies that can easily adapt products to appeal to market niches. As long as the models have meaningful differences and the boundaries around the niches are real and sustainable, total sales volume correlates with the number of models produced.

The market segments of the automobile industry are widely discussed, but even in mature industrial markets like machine tools there is the opportunity to gain share by developing models offering different trade-offs among ease of setup, throughput, flexibility, and price. Making products aimed at these niches means going through the commercialization process not just once but three and four times and incorporating incremental changes—not necessarily big breakthroughs—in each new release.

Leading companies serve many more market segments than do followers. Over a ten-year period, Casio, the industry leader in the Japanese market for hand-held calculators, introduced 2.5 times as many products as Sharp, the follower. In the world market for point-and-shoot 35mm cameras, the gap between leader and follower is now two times. In mid-range UNIX computer systems, the gap is nearly four times.

## BREADTH OF TECHNOLOGIES

In many markets, products incorporate an increasing number of technologies, and companies must be able to master—or to acquire and integrate—all of them if they are to compete. The copier market illustrates the point.

Ten years ago, copiers simply coordinated the light source and a toner system with a moving piece of paper, requiring technology for three things: to mechanically move the paper, to coordinate and focus the lens and the light source, and to apply and fuse toner. Competing in that market meant pushing for innovation in mechanical paper movement, optics, and fusing systems. Competence in those technologies is still needed but is no longer enough. Companies also need to be at the cutting edge of other technology areas: control hardware and software, organic photoreceptors, and panel displays. Companies that fall behind in any one area risk producing an uncompetitive product.

The situation is the same in many industries. Automobiles now include a range of new control electronics, braking systems, structural materials, and engine materials. Semiconductors involve innovations not just in process technology but also in packaging, testing, and

interconnect technologies. Manufacturers of DRAMs
have had to keep up with ever more complex production
processes. The number of process steps needed to manufacture state-of-the-art DRAMs has increased from 230
in 1985 to 550 today, and the variety of equipment
needed for manufacture has risen 20%. Even in pharmaceuticals, which has always been interdisciplinary, the
need to stay current in chemical, biological, and biomedical technologies has grown over the past ten years as
understanding of disease mechanisms and genetic engineering has grown.

## Building Commercialization Capability

The best commercializers do more than understand the
importance of getting the right product to the market
repeatedly and quickly. They take steps to ensure that
the organization can achieve that result reliably and
quickly, even if it means changing the way they do business. Canon's efforts typify the manner in which high-
performing companies strengthen their commercialization capability.

Canon is widely recognized as a leader in optical and
imaging technologies, electronics assembly, software,
and high-precision assembly of small parts. It has used
this leadership to build and grow successful businesses
in cameras, copiers, office automation, and medical
equipment. The company's revenues have grown as a
result, from ¥ 200 billion in 1981 to ¥ 1 trillion in 1988.
In 1981, Canon was about the same size as Nikon. It is
now four times as large.

Canon had always valued its ability to bring technology to the market, but as competition intensified in the
mid-1980s, company president Ryuzaburo Kaku decided

to act. Shrinking product life cycles and an increasing dependence on suppliers for key subsystems, which competitors could buy as well, led him to conclude that Canon's future lay in becoming a market leader with its own unique technologies. Kaku established superior commercialization as a high priority and expressed that priority in two clear objectives: "winning with our own technology" in optics, electronics, and precision manufacturing and "50% down" (cutting product development cost and time in half). To reinforce these goals, the company built a highly automated lens-grinding plant and created a central lab to feed improved optical technologies to the plant. Management also supported the objective of "50% down" by encouraging divisional managers to be readily accessible to project managers. Everyone in the company learned that delays caused by waiting for management approval were acceptable no longer.

The focus on commercialization capability had different but important effects on the ways Canon's managers thought and acted. The semiconductor-equipment division, which produces photolithographic systems, was already skilled at commercialization. It had been staffing new project teams with experienced members who could transfer learning from previous projects, organizing primarily around products rather than functions to ease coordination and involving customers in subsystem testing to discover problems early. But the division saw the president's message as a challenge to be even more aggressive. It set the ambitious goal of cutting six months off the development time for new equipment. To achieve that goal, it used computer-aided-design tools to eliminate some phases of project management, and it overlapped other phases.

The streamlined commercialization process cut development costs by 30% and time to market by 50% and enabled the division to launch two generations of equipment in the time it took competitors to introduce one. Canon could also offer upgraded versions of each generation every one-and-a-half years, while its toughest competitor took three years. Canon's share of the world market for photolithographic equipment rose from 16% in 1978 to 25% in 1988. One of its main competitors, which made little effort to strengthen commercialization capability, saw its share drop from 51% to 23% in the same period.

Canon's camera division also revitalized its commercialization processes. In 1985, Minolta challenged Canon's top standing in the market for 35mm single-lens-reflex cameras by launching the first autofocus model, which incorporated novel electronic controls and a miniaturized motor. The model opened a whole new market of consumers who wanted the sharpness of 35mm photographs without having to master complex focus controls. Minolta quickly followed up the original autofocus model with two different models aimed at smaller segments of the new market. And by 1986, with 36% of the market, Minolta eclipsed Canon as the 35mm market leader.

Spurred by top management's call for aggressive action and drawing on the company's research in optics, Canon's camera division retaliated by introducing two products that exploited a breakthrough in lens technology: sonically driven motors mounted in the lens to allow 50% faster focusing. By the end of 1986, Canon had pulled even with Minolta, and over the next 15 months it battled to remain at the top by hammering out three other models that covered additional segments.

To strengthen their commercialization capability,
high-performers like Canon do the following: make commercialization capability a top-management priority; set
goals to focus the effort; develop skills; and get managers
directly involved in the commercialization process to
speed actions and decisions.

## MAKE COMMERCIALIZATION A PRIORITY

However obvious it seems, top managers at successful
companies explicitly put commercializing technology
high on the corporate agenda. Average performers fail
to make this simple effort, sometimes because they
equate commercialization with R&D and think they can
improve it by spending more money. But consider the
fate of one high-technology company whose top managers recognized the importance of commercialization
but failed to make it an explicit priority.

In the mid-1980s, this U.S. semiconductor company
was performing well. Its revenues and profits had been
growing steadily. In several of its markets, it controlled
nearly 50% of the business, and it had excellent relationships with its leading customers. By 1986, however, the
U.S. semiconductor industry was in a worldwide competitive struggle, and this company was in the thick of it.
After much thought and debate, top management pro-
mulgated a set of initiatives designed to maintain the
company's leadership position.

The initiatives emphasized improved quality, world-
class manufacturing, and excellent customer service.
The managers consciously decided not to include commercialization, innovation, or technological leadership
on the list of corporate priorities. They thought those
objectives were obvious. As the CEO explained, "We felt

that better use of technology and more effective product development was the essence of our business. We're a high-tech company, after all. We didn't need to put those priorities on the list."

Over the next three years, though, the company began to slip. Margins declined, and market shares fell in several businesses the company had once dominated. Top management assigned task forces to study the failing businesses, and in each case, the findings were the same: the competition was "out-commercializing" them. Competitors were marketing more products in a shorter time, developing a lead in new product and process technology, gaining share, increasing their margins, and feeding money back into their commercialization efforts.

In 1989, the besieged semiconductor company amended its corporate priorities and put leadership in technology commercialization at the top of the list. In retrospect, the CEO says that overlooking that priority in 1986 was the worst decision he had made in his 25-year career. He now emphasizes whatever is fundamental to the business, not just what needs the most improvement.

This company's problems are understandable, given the way organizations work. People at lower levels of the organization are not privy to discussions among top executives and have no way of knowing why things are or are not on the priority list. They naturally direct their resources toward studying, training for, and measuring progress against top management's explicit objectives.

If commercialization is truly important, business leaders must send clear signals. Canon's corporate goal of "winning through our own technology" and Hewlett-Packard's objective of "making a needed and profitable contribution" sound innocuous but are actually important drivers of behavior at all levels of these organizations.

## SET GOALS AND BENCHMARKS

Simply identifying superior commercialization capability as a priority does not suffice. Leaders of successful commercializers also translate this priority into objectives others can act on, and they create incentives for them to do so. For instance, they specify key technologies in which the company must lead or set targets for price or product features, and they spur action by making those goals aggressive.

When Canon was developing its personal copier, it aimed for copy quality as good as that of IBM's office copiers, a price of less than $1,500—as opposed to $3,000 for the lowest priced model on the market—and a weight below 20 kilograms—versus 35 kilograms for the lightest competing model. Because the goals were so specific, the project team knew exactly what it had to accomplish. Because the goals were aggressive, managers were forced to find novel ways to reach them. They looked everywhere for opportunities: product and process design, manufacturing, marketing, and service. The management team achieved the quality, price, and weight goals in part by developing a replaceable module that combined critical parts of the image-transfer and fusing systems and by going outside Canon and the copier industry for technology to manufacture the module.

Establishing benchmarks based on competitors' products is another good way to encourage managers to improve the commercialization process. Information about competitors is widely available, and companies that are good at commercializing technology routinely use it to advantage. Customers, suppliers, employees hired from competitors, and joint-venture partners can provide valuable insight into how other companies are performing. Companies should track data on the four dimensions that measure commercialization capability—time to market, range of markets, number of products, and breadth of technologies—as well as cost, delivery time, and service.

When a company that makes a filtering device for radio-transmission equipment wanted to know how it compared with competitors, it went directly to its suppliers and asked, "How are we as a client?" The vendor responded, "You guys are hard to do business with. You overspecify and overconstrain us, so it costs us more." The company subsequently improved its relationship with the supplier and cut its costs by allowing the supplier to do more of the component-design work.

Several Xerox managers credit competitive benchmarking with producing the shock that created the will and energy the company needed to overhaul its copier business in the early 1980s. The analysis forced Xerox to realize that, compared with competitors, its design cycles were long, its technologies old, and its product line limited.

Hewlett-Packard's use of competitive benchmarks saved it in at least one product market. Its radio-frequency analyzer dominated the market, but when H-P engineers tore down a competing Japanese product, they discovered that it was superior to their own design. While H-P used separate wires to connect components, the Japanese company had redesigned the chassis to allow the use of a wire harness to replace separate connections. This difference in design made the Japanese product cheaper and more reliable than H-P's own, more popular, product. H-P quickly turned its attention to improving its design and was able to preserve its market position.

While successful commercializers use goals and benchmarks, they are careful to select only a handful and to use the same ones for several years. In a turn-around effort, one troubled company set 25 challenging goals, but because managers down the line could not follow up on all of them, they made little progress on any one of them. The company abandoned all 25 within a year. Honda, on the other hand, set a single goal for the team that developed the City car for the Japanese market—"Do something different enough to capture the youth market"—and stuck with it for three years, frequently sending the project team back to its drawing boards. This demanding, enduring goal eventually drove the team to develop the "tall boy" concept: a car shorter, taller, and lighter than most, a packaging concept that promised a roomy interior, superior acceleration, and miserly fuel consumption. Both the initial City car and a follow-on turbocharged model were big hits.

## BUILD CROSS-FUNCTIONAL SKILLS

People cannot improve the commercialization process without the necessary skills. High-performing companies emphasize a set of skills notably different from their less successful counterparts. They value cross-functional skills, while other companies pride themselves on their functional strengths. High performers boast, "We've got the best project managers in the world." Low performers say, "We've got the best circuit designers."

Building excellent cross-functional skills is a challenge, especially because structures and habits work against them. People identify with their profession and usually want to get better at what they do. And most day-to-day work is function-specific.

But functional excellence alone does not ensure that a company will be competitive. Compare the testing procedures of a European pharmaceuticals company with that of its U.S. partner. The two companies had entered a joint venture to develop and market a particular drug, but the European company kept falling behind in the development cycle. The drug required two tests—one chemical, one biomedical. The European company was effective in both areas, but separate groups of people in buildings three miles apart conducted the tests. There was little communication between them, and no one took responsibility for coordinating their efforts.

The U.S. company, on the other hand, organized its activity not by scientific discipline but by development phase. It had one manager assigned to oversee the development process, and it performed the testing in one lab with one group of researchers. While the slower company needed six weeks to complete the chemical analysis, the faster company took just three days. The European partner had so much trouble changing its testing procedures that it actually found it more expedient to send samples to the United States and get results shipped back to Europe.

Many companies try to smooth the transitions between separate functions through programs like "design for manufacturability," which links R&D and manufacturing, or "quality function deployment," which links marketing and manufacturing. Superior commercializers also use these programs, but they go far beyond them. They strive to build an extensive network connecting R&D, manufacturing, sales, distribution, and service, and they organize around products, markets, or development phases rather than functions. For them, cross-functional teams are standard practice.

Training can go a long way in blurring functional lines and easing coordination. When Epson, the Torrance, California high-tech manufacturer, was preparing to develop its first personal copier, it sent the mechanical engineer assigned to lead the project back to school for two years of electrical engineering courses.

Job rotation is another way to cross-train. Companies that transfer design engineers to the factory floor during production ramp-up find that it lessens the finger-pointing between them and the manufacturing engineers. Other companies rotate engineers throughout their careers. At NEC, another good commercializer, fewer than half the engineers who start in the research department remain there after ten years. The rest are scattered across various functions within the same business unit.

## PROMOTE HANDS-ON MANAGEMENT TO SPEED ACTIONS AND DECISIONS

Priorities tend to fade if high-level managers don't act on them. At high-performing companies, top managers maintain a visible presence to reinforce the importance of commercialization. Regardless of the company's management style, executives must be interventionist if the rest of the organization is to take commercialization seriously. Even at companies like 3M and Hewlett-Packard that are known for being decentralized and divisionalized, management feels free to go in and meddle in issues crucial to the commercialization process.

It is impossible to guarantee that the organization will always do the right things, but asking hard questions and demanding honest answers about technical performance, cost, and alternative technologies can help prevent big mistakes. Managers at one successful European electronics company ask questions throughout the development cycle: When will the proposed product's price-performance ratio make it competitive with existing technologies? How far down the road is the technology, and how much money do we need to push it into the market? Where could we go wrong? What's the evidence for that conclusion?

Senior managers at high-performing companies promote commercialization in other ways as well—by acting as tiebreakers for disputes at the project level, keeping up to date on the progress of key commercialization efforts, clearing their calendars when serious problems arise, speeding decision making, and making sure the right people and the right information come together. When comparing two quite similar office equipment companies, we observed that senior managers at the company that demonstrated stronger commercialization capability were able to resolve project-level disputes in as little as one day. Senior managers at the other company took up to six weeks to make such decisions.

Inspired genius and scientific breakthroughs will remain essential elements in competitive success. But they are not enough. Increasingly, competitive success hinges on the coordinated efforts of scientists, engineers, manufacturing staff, and marketers building on breakthroughs with ongoing improvements in products and processes. This might mean redesigning a machine tool to incorporate a new motor to serve a new application and doing so faster than competitors, even when the motor was not developed in-house.

Consistently out executing competition on this dimension—being better at commercializing technology—requires a disciplined approach. Improvement starts with top management setting the right priorities along with ambitious goals. Then management throughout the company must follow through with initiatives to build cross-functional skills and to remove obstacles to quick decisions and actions on commercialization projects. Those companies that take this approach will prosper. Those that do not will fall by the wayside.

## About the Study

THIS STUDY OF COMMERCIALIZATION was conceived and conducted by McKinsey & Company to better understand the difference between leaders and laggards in commercializing technology and the links between improved commercialization and competitive success.

To formulate hypotheses to test, McKinsey commissioned a survey of the academic and management literature and reviewed its client work in this area. Then, between December 1988 and April 1989, McKinsey interviewed managers at 19 companies in the United States, Europe, and Japan to find out how they commercialize technology. The number of interviews at each company ranged from as many as 50 to as few as 5, and interviews were conducted with managers at all organizational levels, from chairman to first-line supervisor. The companies were selected to include leaders and laggards in commercialization in industries where commercialization is important, where many companies compete, and where competitive leadership has changed hands in the last decade.

The authors would like to acknowledge the assistance of their colleagues Lorraine Harrington and Roland Worlfram, who conducted many of the interviews and contributed to the analysis; Richard Foster, who guided the effort with his experience and advice and helped shape the conclusions; and Charles Ferguson of MIT's Center for Technology, Policy, and Industrial Development, who conducted the literature search. The authors also appreciate the cooperation and advice throughout this project of the Council on Competitiveness and its chairman, John Young.

# The Commercialization Process

COMMERCIALIZATION BEGINS WHEN a business identifies a way to use scientific or engineering advances to meet a market need. The process continues through design, development, manufacturing ramp-up, and marketing, and includes later efforts to improve the product. While it is often viewed as a linear process—a series of steps performed by people in different functions—companies with strong commercialization capability see the process as a series of overlapping phases that involve many business functions simultaneously. (See figure on next page.)

Take Hewlett-Packard's development of the DeskJet printer. In the mid-1980s, H-P's Vancouver, Washington division, which specializes in printers for personal computers, needed a blockbuster. Market research had shown that PC users would welcome a relatively slow-speed device that printed as clearly as a laser printer but sold for less than half the $2,000 price. In late 1985, a team of researchers, engineers, and marketers formed to explore the feasibility of such a product.

In conceptualizing the product, the team defined customers' needs precisely and clarified the drawbacks of existing low-cost printers. It sized up the proposed product's technical feasibility by reviewing H-P's thermal-ink-jet technology, which uses electrical current to vaporize ink and shoot it onto paper in patterns of microscopic dots. Although earlier printers using that technology required specially coated paper and created narrow, blurred characters, the DeskJet team concluded that given sufficient resources, H-P's InkJet Components Operation in Corvallis, Oregon could refine the technology enough to produce patterns as dense and clear as those from a laser printer.

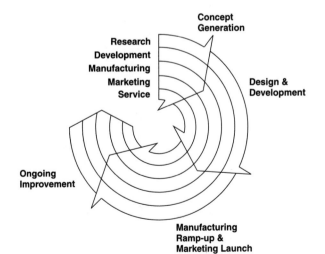

Still in the concept-generation phase, the team brought manufacturing engineers into the process to verify that the company could produce the print head and the printer. Then the team submitted a formal plan, which Vancouver management approved.

Next, the team had to design a manufacturing prototype that could be tested for performance, reliability, producibility, and product cost. It started with a breadboard prototype, an assemblage of components hand-wired to printed circuit boards that represented the technical core of the printer. As soon as the breadboard proved technically feasible and appropriate for the market, H-P augmented its project team with specialists in component sourcing, mechanical design, and control software. Six months later, the expanded group released several working prototypes, complete with cabinet, control software and panel, and paper-handling mechanism, and let consumers try them. The team improved print quality based on feedback from the trials, and the DeskJet was ready for manufacture.

While the DeskJet team was designing and developing the product, the printer factory in Vancouver and the print-head factory in Corvallis had been constructing pilot production lines. At the same time, marketing had developed distribution, promotion, sales, and service plans and had primed the sales force and scheduled an advertising blitz.

H-P officially launched the DeskJet in February 1988—just 26 months after the Vancouver division first explored the idea. It rang up strong sales almost immediately.

Most DeskJet team members transferred to other projects after the launch, but several key engineers and marketers stayed on to oversee ongoing improvements. As customers asked for greater printing speed and more typefaces, the team went back to the concept-generation stage and executed a short version of the commercialization effort. In April 1989, they launched a faster, more flexible, less expensive version of the original printer, and in July 1989, a model that would work with Apple's Macintosh.

**Originally published in May–June 1990**
**Reprint 90310**

# About the Contributors

**AMAR BHIDE** is a visiting professor of entrepreneurship at the University of Chicago, on leave from the Harvard Business School. He is a former senior manager at McKinsey & Company and vice president for proprietary trading at E. F. Hutton. Professor Bhide also served on the staff of the Brady Commission, which investigated the stock market crash of 1987. Among Professor Bhide's publications are *Of Politics and Economic Reality*, eight *Harvard Business Review* articles, and several articles in the *Wall Street Journal*, the *New York Times*, and the *LA Times*. His work on corporate governance includes "The Hidden Costs of Stock Market Liquidity" in the *Journal of Financial Economics* and articles in the *Journal of Applied Corporate Finance*.

**ZENAS BLOCK** has been involved in establishing 28 new businesses, in a variety of roles ranging from lead technical resource to corporate entrepreneur to independent entrepreneur in industries including food processing, cable television, and software. He was the lead founder of the Center for Entrepreneurial Studies at the Stern School, where he was a clinical professor from 1985 to 1994. He is currently an adjunct professor of entrepreneurial management in the school's executive MBA program and serves as an occasional director/adviser/investor for high-potential start-up companies. Professor Block is the project director of the MBA Career Data Project, a nine-university longitudinal study that tracks students entering MBA programs in order to examine relationships between MBA program elements and career outcomes.

IAN C. MACMILLAN is the executive director of the Wharton Entrepreneurial Programs, which consist of the Snider Entrepreneurial Research Center and the Goergen Entrepreneurial Management Programs. He is also the George W. Taylor Professor of Entrepreneurial Studies. Prior to joining the academic world, MacMillan was employed as a chemical engineer and as a scientist at the South African Atomic Energy Board, and gained experience in working with gold and uranium mines, chemical and explosives factories, oil refineries, and soap and food manufacturers. He has served as director of several companies and has had extensive consulting experience. Professor MacMillan's articles have appeared in the *Harvard Business Review,* the *Sloan Management Review,* the *Journal of Business Venturing,* and other journals.

T. MICHAEL NEVENS is a director in McKinsey & Company's Silicon Valley Office. He is a member of the leadership groups of the firm's electronics and multimedia industry practices, and he also serves on the firm's Professional Conduct and Standards Committee. Mr. Nevens consults on a variety of management issues primarily with clients in the computer software, networking, semiconductor, and telecommunications industries. His client-service experience includes work on sales and marketing, R&D, manufacturing, purchasing, the supply chain, organization, and strategy. In addition, he has worked with clients in North America, Europe, and Asia on core business revitalization, new business creation, and market entry as well as on acquisitions, mergers, and alliances. Mr. Nevens's articles have appeared in the *Wall Street Journal,* the *Financial Times,* and the *Harvard Business Review.*

**ARTHUR ROCK** is one of the founders of venture capital and has been a major player in the development of Silicon Valley. Working with Thomas J. Davis, Jr., in the firm Davis & Rock, as well as on his own at Arthur Rock & Co., Mr. Rock has backed many of the companies that make the Valley what it is today: Teledyne, Scientific Data Systems, Apple Computer, General Transistor, and Diasonics, to name of few. He now spends much of his time serving on corporate and nonprofit boards.

**WILLIAM A. SAHLMAN** is the Dimitri V. D'Arbeloff–Class of 1955 Professor of Business Administration at the Harvard Business School. His research focuses on the investment and financing decisions made in entrepreneurial ventures at all stages of their development. He is chairman of the board for the Harvard Business School Publishing Corporation, which conducts all external publishing activities through the *Harvard Business Review*; the Harvard Business School Press; and the case studies, management production, and interactive media groups. From 1990 to 1991, he was chairman of the Harvard University Advisory Committee on Shareholder Responsibility. He is a member of the board of directors of several private companies.

**JAMES MCNEILL STANCILL** is a professor of finance at the Marshall School of Business at the University of Southern California. He is an expert on the financial management of emerging corporations. He also consults with small businesses, specializing in acquisitions and leveraged buyouts, and serves as an ad hoc reviewer for *Financial Management*. Professor Stancill is an expert in entrepreneurial finance, corporate acquisitions, corporate entrepreneurism, and business in China.

**GREGORY L. SUMME** was named president and chief operating officer of EG&G and elected to the company's board of directors in January of 1998. Until recently, he. was president of AlliedSignal's Automotive Products Group. Mr. Summe has served as president of Aerospace Engines and as president of General Aviation Avionics. Before joining AlliedSignal, he was the general manager of commercial motors at General Electric and a partner at McKinsey & Company. He began his career as a semiconductor design engineer at Mostek.

BRO UTTAL was a technology management specialist at McKinsey & Company. He has written more than 60 articles on innovation, technology management, and new product development. He is also the author of *Total Customer Service: The Ultimate Weapon.*

# Index